A Lady's Memories

Part One

1880 to 1906

(Maud Edith Francis née JACKSON)

ISBN: 978-1-910205-90-7

Printed and Published by

For The Right Reasons

60 Grant St

Inverness

IV3 8BS

fortherightreasons@rocketmail.com

07717457247 01463 718844

Foreword

'When we were standing on Exeter platform I had my first sensation of being a person, a reasoning human being - it is quite clear to me and it happened when the train was shunting back - I felt rather grand and grown up'. Maud Jackson 1888.

I've seen things you people wouldn't believe. Attack ships on fire off the shoulder of Orion. I watched C-beams glitter in the dark near the Tannhäuser Gate. All those moments will be lost in time, like tears in rain. Time to die'.

This quote from the film Blade Runner sums up very well the anguish of death. We don't matter much, but the memories we've had, all those things we've seen, all the beauty and the sheer wonder of being alive, these do matter. Their annihilation is hard to bear.

A Suitcase

These memories would have been lost forever if an ex-policeman, Mike Galleitch, hadn't discovered them in a suitcase and purchased them at an auction in Inverness some years ago.

He brought them to our untidy little office at 60 Grant Street Inverness. We are beginners at publishing, and my colleagues told me there was no money in this book! Well, perhaps not, but it has become a matter of duty for me that Maud Jackson's memories should be retrieved for posterity so that death does not wipe out for ever this high born lady's story.

This is Part One of her memories, from her birth in 1880 to 1906 when she married and went to New Zealand. Her earliest years were spent on a captured ship from Nelson's time, moored in the River Hamoaze off Keyham Dockyard, but after her Mother's untimely death the children moved to Putney, London. where her childhood and schooldays, growing up with her sisters under the tender care of Tem, their nanny, are faithfully recorded. Then Tem took them to stay in many beautiful places to improve their education, from Bognor in Sussex to Bangor in Wales, and thence to Paris and Switzerland, and finishing school in Kassell in Germany, before their final return to Devonport. In Part two you will hear about her marriage and her life in New Zealand.

Maud's description of Bognor goes like this:

'They showed me the "sights" of Bognor, which really are impossible to find. It was a small seaside town with a good beach, and the best "sight" was a crowd of poor London children having a seaside holiday'.

But her description of Chateau D'Oeux, in Switzerland is, more flattering:

'We were very happy there and ran wild, and Kate and I used to swing on the hotel swing at every spare moment, especially after meals. I can remember the grown-ups' astonishment at this, but we did not know what they meant. Swinging was a joy, therefore swing as much as you can. It was fun too, meeting fresh people and speaking French instead of German. I have many happy memories of Chateau D'Oeux. One is of a bank of campanulas growing wild, every variety of height, just a lovely garden of blues. Another is of scrambling up to a little natural rock garden on the slopes of the Gumfluh, a 'jardin des plantes' the Swiss called it, and seeing cyclamen growing wild. And going to another village nearer Gruyère, called Rossinières, and trying to draw a picture of a Swiss house carved all over'.

Maud Jackson aged 14.

If you take some real time out of this busy world to read this memoir you will be helping Maud's great labour of love become worthwhile, and extend for a little while the lifespan of these unique memories before they turn to dust. I hope you will enjoy this first part of the book. If you are a relative I hope you will get in touch. Mike Galleitch and I have added quite a lot of genealogical information which I hope someone might find matches theirs. If your surname is Jackson, Francis or Vickers and your great grandfather or great great Uncle was an admiral, or Mayor of Waimate in New Zealand (see part two) or owned Tulloch Castle in Dingwall, Ross-shire, or was called Clifford Coffin and won a VC (see part two), you may well be related! R.B.

Richard Burkitt
Director
For the Right Reasons
Printing and publishing
60 Grant St
Inverness
IV3 8BS
fortherightreasons@rocketmail.com
Mobile Tel 07717 457247

Living in a Boat

I was born on April the 4th 1880 at No. 8 Napier Street, Stoke Damerel.

Stoke Damerel is a suburb of Devonport, England, and Napier Street a little street. I arrived at 12.15 a.m. My father was asleep on the sofa, and being deaf as well as sleepy, thought that the doctor said that I was a boy. The doctor's son was born just before I came and no doubt the doctor was talking about <u>his</u> son. Father was very pleased to have another boy, and wrote to his mother about his mathematical family - boy, girl - boy, girl - boy, girl - and I, the seventh child was a boy and was to be called 'Paul Robert Alexander'. I once read that letter and wish I had it. My eldest sister Helen told me that I was called 'Arthur Knyvett' before I was born, after my father's great friend Admiral Sir A. K. Wilson. Father used to say that Mother and the doctor deceived him! He found out his mistake a few days later. He was then a Commander in the Navy and was in command of the training ships HMS *Lion* and HMS *Implacable*, which were moored together in the Hamoaze off Keyham Dockyard.

The two ships were still there when we were living in Devonport Dockyard in 1899-1902, but were then moored fore and aft so they did not swing with the tide. We lived in the Captain's quarters of the *Implacable* - she was originally a French ship, the *Duguay-Trouin,* and was taken prisoner at the Battle of Trafalgar and renamed. She is still afloat but is kept now (I believe in Falmouth harbour) as an historical ship. The first part of my life was spent on board her. Father always called me 'Seagull', and the nickname started because he never knew if it was the baby or the seagulls crying. Helen told me that the sailors taught me to walk when I was a year old by holding out signaling flags for me. I have seen my quarters. It must have been uncomfortable for my Mother. The cabins are small, and in May 1881 when Kate was born on board there were eight of us children. Kate was named Duguay Trouin after the ship and was rather proud of her name although so few people could pronounce it, and the clergyman at Weybridge, who prepared us for confirmation, said that he hoped he would not have to marry her for he could not say her name. There is a statue of Admiral Duguay Trouin in the courtyard at Versailles, and also one at Toulon or Marseilles - I forget which, but remember that she and father found another statue of her namesake. I cannot remember the *Implacable* when we lived on board. I was christened at Saint James the Less, Keyham.

We had an old coxswain at Devonport Dockyard who could remember being on duty at the steps of Keyham Dockyard when nurses and babies and prams were rowed ashore, and he helped to pull the prams up the landing steps - I can remember the prams - there was a wide one which held two children side by side, and this was the one that Kate and I were in when Father took us out, and he let the pram run by itself and it turned over with Kate underneath and she cut her head - and he did not dare tell Mother that it was because he let go the handle. The other pram held one child and I can remember sitting on the foot part when we were out. We did not take a pram away when we left Devonport and yet we needed one for our legs got very tired walking with the older children. Our legs were weak and we went for long walks and got very tired, and then we would have to have our legs and feet bathed in 'Tidman's Sea Salt' every morning after our bath.

I can remember living in Napier Street, but nothing much about it. Mrs Olding used to say 'The house is not nice enough for Mother. Not nice enough for her'. Mother was an only daughter and had an income from £10,000. She lived at 6 Collingwood Villas at Stoke before I was born. I think that Charlie, Esther, Harold and Esmé were born there. Tom was born at Plymouth and Helen in London, the only one of us not born in Devonshire. I can remember being with Mother, sleeping in her room, putting on white socks in her room, having breakfast with her when she gave me little squares of bread and butter, looking out of the dining room window with her to see Esmé start off to kindergarten, Esmé wearing a dark green coat with a cape and a bow of ribbon at the back - standing by Mother's knee in the drawing room when someone gave me a silver locket (the someone was my Godmother Geraldine O' Neill). She called on us once when I was over twenty, but never wrote or paid any attention to me and I know nothing about her except that she was slim and nice looking. I remember mother picking me up when I fell downstairs and telling me not to cry because there was a man in the dining room - who he was and why he must not be disturbed I do not know, except that I was shrieking. I can remember seeing two brown heads on the pillows in Mother's bed when I stood up in my cot.

Best of all I can remember Mother taking Harold, Kate and me in a steamer to Saltash. Kate was dressed in white and sat on Mother's lap and Harold was so thin that Mother laughed and said he must not fall through the railings into the harbour. That is a very bright and clear memory of a moment, it must have been sunny. There was a green lawn sloping down to the river where we went, and a white fox terrier playing on the lawn. I must have been three then or younger, and when I described it to Father years later he said the place was Saltash and the garden was Marshall Fiske's garden. Marshall Fiske was Father's Mother's brother or cousin and she always used to 'snort' if he were mentioned, for she dearly loved her other brother Frederic Fiske who died as a young man. They are both in the family silhouette group of the Fiskes in 1828.

Mother dies

From photographs of Mother she had curly brown hair parted in the middle; very large brown eyes, a wide kind good face and she was good-looking too. Her eyes and brow are so sad and pathetic. Mrs Olding told me that she was never strong and always having babies and always being ill. Her last illness was dreadful, she died of cancer of the breast when she was 38, leaving 8 children, the eldest 16 and the youngest 3. She had a long illness and was (taken) away from us. Gertrude Smith, (my cousin Gertrude Blomfield Jackson) remembers Mother staying with them at Rothbury House, Upper Richmond Road, Putney, for a long time and was very fond of her. Gertrude was fourteen when Mother died, so old enough to know about her tragic illness. Uncle George's surgeon brother Marcus Beck was consulted. I do not know if he operated, but there was an operation as Gertrude remembers that mother could not do her hair afterwards. Father told us that the most dreadful thing he had ever had to do was to tell Mother that she was going to die. Up to then the doctors had been optimistic to Mother, hoping that it would help a cure. She died in a nursing home at Blackheath. When the end was near we three 'little ones', Esmé 6, me 4 and Kate 3, were taken to say goodbye. We were told to be very quiet, and we whispered so quietly that Mother could not hear us. She was in a high bed up above my eyes. At the foot of the bed was a little table with the grapes and butterscotch on it, which I hoped was for us - and it was. I can remember seeing Mother's face on the pillow, but not any feeling of sadness. Of course we did not know what it all meant, never having experienced death. Father put us into the train when we left, perhaps he came with us, and I can see him now standing by the open door of the railway carriage. He had a brown beard and I loved him very much. He always petted me, and as he did not leave us until I was 6, when he went to the North American and West Indian Squadron as Captain of the *Comus,* I have endless memories of him. I have been told that when I was very small Mother took the rest of the family to stay at Looe, and Father would have to cross the Hamoaze and wheel me in my pram for miles over rough hilly roads.

Stoke Newington Rectory with Grandparents

When Mother died the Devonport home was at an end. Our nurse had taken us to stay with our Grandparents at the Rectory, Stoke Newington, in North London. Father was stationed in London as Naval Adviser to the War Office. The older ones were at school or with friends and Tom was in the Navy. Helen went to boarding school. Charlie and Harold went to Preparatory School at Mannamead. Esther could not go to school as she had had scarlet fever very badly when she was 8 and we were living on board the *Implacable*. The ship's doctor took her to the Naval Hospital at Stonehouse and nursed her himself. Sick men used to be rowed from their ships to the Naval Hospital. I wonder if they are still taken that way. Esther recovered, although a good many rules of naval discipline must have been broken, and was sent back to her day school. I do not know what happened, but she next got some form of brain fever which left her with St Vitus dance, poor child.

We children never noticed her jerks and jumps, at least we took them as a matter of course and she got better when she was older. Our Nanny Mrs Olding looked after us that summer. I must here explain who Mrs Olding was. She was a Devonshire girl, Mary E. Bunce, and used to say 'My Grandmother was a Rendell'. Then Mary Bunce married Mr Benjamin Smythe Olding, a widower with no children, well to do and 'something in the City'. I have forgotten just what. He had very thick hair and a beard and it was snow white when he was 21. He was 25 years older than her. She was always pretty and had a wonderful little svelte figure and wore 'Princess' dresses to perfection. She never had any children. She was one of the best and kindest friends I have ever had and I loved and admired her and respected her. No family of motherless children ever had a more wonderful friend. She was always called Mrs. Olding but she was like the kindest of aunts.

To go back to the Stoke Newington Rectory - we three travelled from Devonport with our nurse. I can see Kate sitting on her lap pulling a yellow rose to pieces. When the train stopped at Exeter we got out to go to the lavatory and when we came back to the platform the train had started towards the arch of the tunnel. The guard had locked our carriage. He stopped the train and we were put in the carriage again. Curiously enough, when we were standing on Exeter platform I had my first sensation of being a person, a reasoning human being - it is quite clear to me and it happened when the train was shunting back - I felt rather grand and grown up.

Not that trains were such a novelty, for our housemaid at Devonport was engaged to a porter, and I had been to the station with her and sat in grandeur in an empty carriage being shunted. I was invited to the engine but thought it would be dirty. I was wearing a cream pelisse trimmed with little silky squiggles all over it!

Mother must have taken great pains over our clothes, such beautifully made baby clothes were divided between her five daughters and I still have some for my daughters. Her Mother had been in India before she was born, and her father lived and died there, which may account for the very fine muslin baby clothes.

I have wandered away from the Rectory again. I remember nothing more of the journey, but that night I fell out of bed and enormous people came with a candle and put me back. The relations at the Rectory were our grandparents and two aunts and an uncle. Grandfather was the Reverend Prebendary Thomas Jackson M.A. Oxon. and Grandmother was Elizabeth Prudence Fiske, the girl with the piece of sugar in the silhouette picture. The aunts were Aunt Nora, Honoria Tufuell Jackson, who is still alive (Feb 1940) and Aunt Ada Frances Broughton Jackson, born in Sydney in 1851, who afterwards married a Mr Tower. I cannot remember the uncle being there so perhaps he was away; he was Uncle Fred, the youngest of that family and a very dear person.

Grandfather was ill then, in 1884, and we were not supposed to go into his room. Kate and I went in against orders. He was sitting in a chair, dressed in black, and we reached up and tucked little sweets into his mouth. He had a wide straight mouth like Aunt Nora's. We were not found out, but we knew he liked us although I don't think he spoke. We were right; he always loved children and animals as I have often heard my aunts say. He died in March 1886.

We were put into deep mourning when Mother died and our red cashmere frocks were dyed black, which I thought a dreadful thing to do as the red was so pretty. We wore black for ages. In the oil painting of me when five (painted by Tem) I was wearing a black dress and black snood. In the photographs taken of Kate and me for Father when he went away in 1886 I am wearing a black dress and black sailor's hat, and Kate a grey dress. We were aged five and six then.

Our home in Putney, London, with Nanny Tem

Our next home was at 15 Disraeli Road, Putney, London, only a few minutes' walk from where Uncle Blomfield and Aunt Bessy lived, and their children Arthur, Gertrude, Dolly and Gilbert, all older than me.

Tem took charge of us, and we had a new nurse, a nice tall fair girl called Blanche. We liked the change; we did not like the other nurse. How can I describe Tem? She was thirty seven then, and had been a friend of Mother's who wanted to take care of us. What an undertaking – to 'mother' eight children and manage her brother's house on a small income. She had to give up her painting which was her chief interest, and her travels abroad with her well to do Cousin Elizabeth Fiske. Tem is short for Aunt Emily. I think my eldest brother Tom gave her the name when he was a little boy. She was always Tem or Temmy to us, or Temmy darling. She looked after us for years. We went to Putney in 1884, and left in October 1893. By that time Tom, Charlie and Harold were all at sea, and Helen and Esther had gone in November 1892 to Jamaica where Father was Commodore of the dockyard. Tem took Esmé, Kate and me to Kassel in Germany that October of 1893, and we stayed there until 1895. In the summer of 1894 she took us to Switzerland and to the Black Forest. In July 1895 we went to Switzerland again and in September of that year we went to Paris. In January 1896 Esmé joined our Father and our stepmother Marian and went to the south of France, and Tem took Kate and me back to England where we went to boarding school and parted from her. So she 'Mothered' us for 11½ years - I was 15¾ then and Kate a year younger.

She was a wonderful person in many ways, but must have found us very tiresome and I don't think she influenced the older ones much. She always did her duty, made and mended our clothes, devoted herself to us all the time, read out loud, encouraged and helped with lessons, and I have heard her say that she tried to keep up Mother's ways and not to make changes or annoy the older ones. She was very tidy and clean and methodical, had no idea of dressing herself, but then she never spent an unnecessary penny on herself, but she dressed us as best she could on a small income. Aunt Bessy told me that 'Tem slaved for you children'. She interested us in many things, in her 'district' of poor people, in painting, in loving good pictures, in books. She always looked up anything she did not know and was always educating herself. Then she was nice and plump, and always had a comfy lap ready for a tired child. She disapproved of lots of things, and as we got older Kate and I used to tease her so as to hear the disapprovals, but she never minded. She was a good Churchwoman and very loyal and always went to church. She used to read the Bible to the three youngest ones (we were called the little ones) on Sundays after lunch in the drawing room. I had to learn the Collect, Esmé and Kate something else. I never understood why we could not all learn the same. Occasionally she would let us choose the Bible story, but we always chose the Ten Plagues of Egypt, and she used to look disapproving, but would read it.

When she was young she studied at South Kensington and made many artist friends. She was chosen from the students to teach the three elder daughters of the Duke of Edinburgh, Queen Victoria's second son. She taught drawing very well, her 'perspective' being very good; in fact she could teach better than paint, although the constant interruptions to her painting probably caused this. She also knew anatomy, bones and muscles, better than most doctors! She also loved botany. Whenever any of her relations or friends wanted to know anything they asked Tem for the information, for if she did not know she would always find out for them.

The house at Disraeli Road was a semi-detached one, built of yellow brick, with a little front garden, a green front door and an asphalt path to the back door which was at the side of the house. There was no basement.

Disraeli Road

The drawing room was by the front door and had a bow window; behind it was the dining room which had French windows leading to the back garden. The kitchen, scullery and two lavatories were down a passage past the staircase. There were two or three cellars under the kitchen. Over the kitchen and scullery was a room which was Tem's studio when not wanted as a bedroom, and a bathroom and a lavatory. A short flight of stairs led to two bedrooms and a dressing room. Up again were two bedrooms over the studio and a short flight of stairs led to two more large bedrooms and one small one over the dressing room. The furniture was all very plain and shabby and well worn. No plush curtains or Nottingham lace curtains at the windows, any more than there were rows of geraniums, lobelias and calceolarias in the garden, for Tem thought those fashions frightful, even if they could have been afforded. Oil portraits of our great-grandparents, Mr and Mrs Alexander, and of our grandmother Mrs Gordon, hung in the dining room, and there was a bookcase decorated with a variety of carvings. Mrs Gordon was pretty and I liked the bookcase and read all the books. Otherwise the dining room was dark and depressing to me. The drawing room was light and I liked it but thought it plain compared to the heavily upholstered drawing rooms of some of our friends. Mrs Bright, daughter-in-law of the famous John Bright, had blue velvet curtains in her drawing room which I thought quite lovely. But I hated screens with scarves hanging over them and sham spiders and mantelpieces all covered with heavy stuff, which was the fashion.

Our drawing room had white muslin curtains with frills, a polished floor and shabby carpet, an old gilt mirror over the mantelpiece which was whitish marble, and on the mantelpiece stood the bronze storks and carved ivory that Father brought from China when he was a Midshipman. An inlaid table made a writing table and on it stood the photograph of Tem's Three Princesses (which I have now). On the wall opposite the fireplace was a funny old chiffonier, full of china and ivory chessmen, and on top of it stood a collection of birds in a glass case. I think there were two glass cases of birds and one of a little white Jap dog somewhere in the house which had belonged to Mother, probably treasures of her Mother's. Not Tem's taste anyway. There was an upright piano with rose coloured silk fluting across the front. By the fireplace there were two armchairs covered in faded chintz, and I can remember peeping underneath the chintz and seeing cross stitch work - how I would love to have those chairs now! There were two coloured drawings of our great aunts, Annie and Helen Alexander, who died young, and one or two of Tem's engravings of Italian old masters. There was a table in the middle of the room covered with an embroidered tablecloth, probably Armenian work which had lots of chain stitch, and on this stood the lamp and some books.

The small garden had a privet hedge to hide the scullery. Beyond this was an oblong of grass, and around this a gravel path with narrow flower beds on each side, and at the bottom of the garden was a shed called the fowl shed, but no fowls were ever there. We each had our own patch of garden and grew what we liked, and Tem kept it all gay all the summer with annuals.

Disraeli Road was an ugly street of semi-detached houses. The houses opposite were smaller than ours and behind them was the railway line from Waterloo. Our street led into the High Street and near the corner were some livery stables where one could see the horses being fed and groomed. I never liked

Putney, the smuts and dirt of London was depressing and the winter fogs made me ill. We went for walks every day until schooldays started, generally going to the Common which was rather a long walk for small children.

In 1886 Father left the War Office and went to the North America and West Indies Station as Captain of the *Comus.* He had a brown beard then, and I remember we saw him off at Putney Station and I was lifted up to kiss him through the window.

That summer Tem took me, and Esther too, to Lodsworth in Sussex and we stayed at a farmhouse with a Mr and Mrs Hurst. It was all pure beauty to me. I loved everything except the cows - the farmyard was interesting and there was a cherry tree outside our sittingroom window and a honeysuckle in the hedge.

In 1887 Esmé and I had measles, and when we were well Tem took us to Cowes. Her princesses were staying at Osborne, and she gave them their drawing lessons there. Helen joined us at Cowes. She had been in France after leaving her boarding school at Forest Hill. Cowes was gay and crowded and the houses were decorated for the regatta. One house was covered with yellow paper roses, really very pretty.

I learned to sew when I was six, and made clothes for my doll in tiny stitches, and the same year, 1886, started violin lessons with Miss Green. She used to scold me for not looking at the music but I wanted to play by ear. So I learned music reading before the ABC! Tem taught me to read later that year, first from a very elementary reading book and then from a story called 'Our White Violet'.

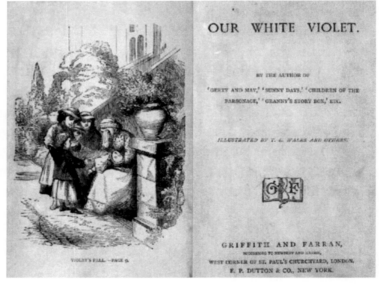

She started to read this to me, then left off, and as nobody in the house would read out loud to me I mastered reading in no time so as to find out what happened to Violet the heroine. Helen sometimes gave me lessons, her idea being long, long columns of figures to add up. If I did all of my lessons I had a halfpenny a week, and I can remember gladly letting the halfpenny go sooner than struggle over and over again with those addition sums. Helen was so clever, and I never could do maths and all lessons had to be plodded through. I was the complete donkey of the family about sums, in fact I must have been a queer fish, for I was the only one who liked dolls and cried easily and liked to be quiet, and hated to be teased.

School in Putney

I went to school in the autumn of 1887; aged 7½ years, to the upper class of the Kindergarten of the South West London Girls' School, Miss Sandell and Miss Redpath, headmistresses, and Miss McKay was Kindergarten mistress, one of those square, straight haired just woman that children can depend on. She taught us to be very tidy and to try hard over our lessons. We had drilling and games to music and everything had to be 'just so' a là Miss Holderness. I can't remember any fusses in her schoolroom. There were three classes in that big room. Esmé had been in the Kindergarten before me, but that was before Miss McKay's day, and the teacher in charge then was a frivoller and no disciplinarian. Esmé was so quick and clever and might have done so well at school but she never bothered. She was nervous and excitable and grew fast and was strong and noisy. She always seemed quite old to me although she was only two years older.

Nature study at the Kindergarten consisted of our once collecting frogs' eggs in a pond and keeping them in a bowl and watching the tadpoles hatch, and one day there was a little frog. We also learnt sewing and made grey flannel shirts for poor boys.

I had a great friend called Muriel Hocker who was the same age. When we were 9½ years old we moved into Form 1 of the School and moved up steadily each year. There was another nice girl called Louisa Storey (who has since been headmistress of the School for Officers' daughters at Bath). There was a little group of us who kept together; always rather afraid of the teachers and the older girls of the class, the rule of the school being that if you did not work you were not moved up. A good rule was that if you could not spell or write well you had to continue dictation and handwriting lessons even in the senior forms.

We had no prizes, but there were certificates of the three grades given instead at the end of the summer term. I did not like school and we were certainly overworked, too many dry text books and far too much preparation. Many of the lessons were dreadfully dull. I used to be away in the winter with very bad colds, and then was 'kept in' for not knowing the work. But being kept in meant that a teacher would explain the matter to you and that was a great help. We were kept in after the morning school and after the teacher had had her lunch she would come to you. Then you raced home (we lived only five minutes' walk away) swallow something with Tem and Helen looking as if they thought you must have been naughty, and tear back for afternoon school. We learnt a great many subjects, a few of them being well taught, but only a few - Miss Redpath's literature lessons when she enthused over Shakespeare and Miss Elvey's science lessons and Miss Strong's mathematics. The science was a joy, Miss Elvey would boil water in a glass bowl and show us 'U' tubes and teach us Physical Geography. She was very lame and had such a white fragile face and was a lady. So was Miss Strong, who was young and had red hair and loved her subject. She knew that I struggled to understand her and just couldn't grasp what Algebra was about and was not naughtily stupid about sums and Euclid. She once took me for a walk on the Common to look for trap-door bees, and we found some.

After two years of Miss Green's violin teaching I learnt from Herr Schneider at school. He always wore a frock coat and an overcoat, and in winter a thick black topcoat as well. He was stout and quite kind and kindly. During Lent, Tem used to take me to some of the Saturday 'Pops', these were popular concerts given on Saturday afternoons and Monday evenings in St. James' Hall, Piccadilly, when if you waited in a queue you could sit in the orchestra chairs for one shilling. We went to Piccadilly in the bus. Joachim (a Hungarian violinist) came to London every Lent and played to you, sometimes alone and also in the famous Quartet Joachim, Riess, Strauss and Piatti. Piatti was the 'cellist, a darling old man rather like a cello himself. It was heavenly music. Sometimes Lady Hallé (Norma Neruda) played too, and I heard Joachim and Lady Hallé play together with Sir Charles Hallé accompanying. There was a wonderful young pianist too, Leonard Borwick. But Joachim towered over them all, his playing was perfect. Sometimes Mary Smith came too (Cousin Arthur Smith) and would take me with her to a Monday 'Pop' and we would sit in the stalls, and she would give me the score of some great concerto or sonata to read. They really were marvellous concerts. Years later when I was at school at Weybridge, Dr Dawes would occasionally take two or three of us to a Monday Pop and one heard that lovely music again. In those pre-gramophone and pre-wireless days it used to make one so enthusiastic and feel as if one should practice for hours and hours every day. Kate followed me to the College but we were never in the same class. Unfortunately Esmé and I were and it was not nice for either of us.

To the Dower House at Lodsworth

In 1888 Tem took Esmé, Kate and me to Lodsworth, and we stayed with Miss Hollist at the Dower House. It had a black and white stone paved hall, and four poster beds, and some of the windows were still bricked up, the result of the 'Window Tax' In the housekeeper's room was an old violin with such a soft tone, not muted but as gentle as a mute, and I was allowed to play on it. The Squire of the Village was Col. Hollist, and we went to Schoolroom tea there, and everyone laughed at the story of how I would not walk past the cows in the park when I was asked to tea with them two years before. The cows were all tethered - but I was six years old and how was I to know that? The cows all looked at me, and I ran back to the farm.

Cowdray Park and the ruins of Cowdray House were close by at Midhurst, and one day we went to Petworth and were shown the state rooms and the pictures by the housekeeper. I remember Petworth quite well, and several of the pictures, especially the portrait of Henry VIII and the Grinling Gibbons carvings. We had picnics in Cowdray Park, and found wild strawberries among the ruins. And we liked the village talk of the Curse of the Monks of Eastbourne at Midhurst, the curse of fire and water when Henry VIII stole their lands. Tem however did not like us to listen to curses or to village gossip.

Father home

Father came home from the West Indies and that was a great joy. He would take us for walks to level crossings and let us swing on the gates - or perhaps it was the signalman who allowed that - and let us hold hands and skip along the pavement. I remember he went away for the Manoeuvres that year, but don't think that he left us again until 1890 when he went to the Mediterranean Fleet as Captain of HMS *Colossus.*

Brothers and sisters and a family picture

Charlie was always away at sea. He had failed in the entrance exam for the Navy and was trained in the *Conway* for the Merchant Service and then made several voyages as an 'apprentice' round the Horn to San Francisco, so we only saw him after long intervals. Charlie was very handsome; he had curly hair and large eyes with very long eyelashes and a clear complexion. He was always so kind to me and I remember his extraordinary good looks when I was still a small girl. Tom and Harold both did brilliantly in the *Britannia.* Tom passed out with five fist classes (highest possible) and Harold passed in first of the candidates, and passed out with five first classes. But Harold lost six months, as the first time he went up he failed in his medical examination, which came before the other examinations. He was a thin delicate boy and sea life must have been hard for him, and he was not too good a sailor either. The last time we were together was in 1888 and we were photographed in a family group - what Tem must have gone through to get us all to the photographers! I wanted to be photographed with my best doll (the one Mother gave to me) so then Kate, who hated dolls, had to take hers too. The big ones did not want to be photographed with dolls. At the last moment Tom put his hat on Esther's head and I saw this (I must have been wriggling too) so did Kate - and in the photograph Kate, Esther and I are all grinning. Tom looks extremely grave. Helen was staring out of a window and sticking out her tongue and you would never know what a very pretty girl she was. Harold is bolt upright trying to look taller than Esmé who at the time was growing very fast. She was only ten and Harold was thirteen.

So at the end of 1892 Tem was left with only 'The three little ones' in the Putney house. In 1888 Uncle Blomfield and Aunt Bessy had left Rothbury House and lived at 29 Mecklenburgh Square until Uncle Blomfield died in 1905. He always called the house 'Meck', a term of endearment. All these relations were so good to us and I loved them all - and still do. Gertrude and Dolly were ten and seven years older and had a knack with children and kept me happy and amused and would take one for walks. Gertrude made my doll some pretty clothes to wear when we went to

Cowes in 1887, and I can still remember one of Doll's long stories called 'The Twenty-Six Children'. They had been to the college too, but left before I went there. In 1889 I stayed at Meck in Dolly's care, and she lent me 'The Prince and the Pauper' by Mark Twain and I thought the whole visit a delight, but she told me in later years that I nearly wore her out and the book was to keep me quiet while she rested.

Life in Putney

When we went to Putney in 1884 it still had old houses in it, as well as all the many streets and shops. I can just remember a few old trees growing in the High Street, their trunks surrounded by paving stones. Our doctor, Dr Shepherd, lived in an old house in the High Street which stood back from the road with a sort of square garden or courtyard in front. Jenny Lind 'The Swedish Nightingale' had lived there. Our friends the Drydens lived in another old house nearer the river on the other side of the High Street, a panelled house with a fine staircase, and a front door opening on the street and a long garden behind.

The Boat Race

Mrs Archibald Smith had a house with a big garden facing on the river, close to where Oxford and Cambridge boat crews had their boatsheds. We saw the start of the Boat Race every year from the garden. There was a high brick wall along the towing path, and seats were erected, so there was a wonderful view looking down on the river and on the crowds. What fun that was and what a crowd. The Archibald Smiths were 'Cambridge' and pale blue flags waved from the big old trees by the high wall, and we were 'Oxford' and wore dark blue rosettes. This garden, and also the old house where the Drydens lived, were covered with small houses many years ago. I can also remember the old wooden bridge, and have an idea that it was a toll gate, but may have got mixed with 'The Halfpenny Gate' between Devonport and Stonehouse. The new bridge was opened in 1886 by the Prince of Wales (King Edward VII) who afterwards drove through Putney and passed by Rothbury House in the Upper Richmond Road. We three little ones were standing on one of the gates of the drive and he gave us a special bow and smile. At least we thought it was for us. Perhaps Uncle Blomfield was behind us and the bow was for him, for Uncle Blomfield was tutor to the Prince of Wales' daughters.

Outside Putney railway station three flowerwomen sat wrapped in shawls with their big baskets of flowers. We each had a favourite flowerwoman and if we had a penny for flowers they would give us such a good pennyworth. I learnt to tell the time for the sake of my flowerwoman. They would ask us to look inside the station at the station clock and tell them the time, and Esmé would do this, which seemed a grand thing to be able to do, so I learned the art to tell my flowerwoman too.

Then you passed the chemist, who had coloured balls in the window and who laughed when one of us asked him for Black Cousin Oranges instead of Black Currant Lozenges; and the confectioner who sold such good pikelets (a type of pancake) and, across the Upper Richmond Road, at the next corner was the French hairdresser who cut our hair, and soon after that Putney Hill began. It was what is called a residential district. Mr Swinburns lived in one of the first houses. He was a short little man who had greyish red hair and walked quickly with both his thumbs sticking out. Our school was two doors past his house. Some of our friends lived in Putney Hill or the side streets, Sir William and Lady White (the Chief Naval Constructor) and the Jeffs (he was a Judge) and Mr and Mrs Smith whose daughter was Mrs George Stevenson. I believe she and Father were engaged, or wanted to be engaged, once. Mr Smith's house was full of pictures, engravings in some rooms, oil paintings in others, and one called 'The Dog in the Manger' interested me - it is a sort of Tate Gallery or Christmas Supplement picture, just what a child likes. The Smiths always gave a children's party on Twelfth Night.

Mrs. Nelson and her two daughters lived in Cambalt Road off Putney Hill and we often went to her house. Father was engaged to Miss Lydia Nelson in 1885 and the engagement was broken off because Father did not go to Communion Service and Miss Nelson felt she ought not to marry a man who was not a Communicant. Aunt Bessy told me this and said also that Miss Nelson never regretted her decision. It did not prevent her from showering kindnesses and treats on us all. She and Tom never hit it off, but neither of them ever criticised the other to us - we knew about the little aloofness of course! Kate and I would go to tea, wearing our best muslin pinafores, and sashes underneath. Directly we go there, Miss Nelson would untie our sashes and tie them on top of the pinafores. She would give us strawberry jam and real tea with lots of sugar in it, and read 'The Three Bears' to us and we loved it all. Mrs Nelson and Miss Annie were sweet and gentle. Miss Nelson always seemed the leader. She had a funny trick of looking at her shoulder constantly, and we were told that this was the result of being in a frightful railway accident with her father in Wales. She had light red hair and very fair skin, was fashionably dressed but always rather 'nervy'. She was very kind to Charlie and Harold and wrote to them when they were away at sea. She ran the Boot Club for the parish, which caused her a lot of work and endless little accounts for the poor who subscribed.

Trip to the Naval Review with Miss Nelson

She once gave me a wonderful treat and took me to the Diamond Jubilee Naval Review at Spithead in 1897. I was at school at Weybridge and she got permission from Dr Dawes to let me be away for four days. We stayed on the Front at Southsea and shared a bedroom. The sittingroom looked over the Front to the ships. We went on board Harold's ship to see the Review and of course I had a marvellously happy day. There was a frightful thunderstorm late that afternoon, the sort you never forget - like the great storm in London soon after Princess Margaret Rose's birth. Most of the tens of thousands of people were soaked but we were lucky, as we were in a carriage at the time. We were on the floating bridge from Gosport to Portsmouth during the worst of the storm and poor Miss Nelson was so frightened - not screamingly so, but really frightened. Our horses were rearing, the bridge was packed with carriages and she was afraid of a carriage pole coming through and killing or hurting one of us. Charlie and Harold were both there and held her hands and comforted her. After the storm that evening the fleet was illuminated, each ship outlined in electric lights and searchlights flashing. It was a lovely sight. Tom was on board his ship too, and some of the relations were his guests and got wet. The larger ships were in the places of honour and Harold's, being only a brig, was at the Gosport end of the long line of ships.

Harold's child Betty is born

Harold was married to Louie (Browne) and Miss Nelson was very fond of Louie, and when Harold went to the Mediterranean Fleet, Louie stayed with Miss Nelson and their first child Betty was born in her house. She turned two rooms into nurseries, and it must have given her great pleasure to have them. Harold did not see Betty until she was two years old. When Miss Nelson died she left legacies to Helen and to my nephew Thomas Sturges Jackson, Charlie's son, who has the same name as Father - a large legacy to Betty and Harold was the residuary legatee. I think she had cousins but no very near relations. I don't think anyone was more surprised than Harold and Louie.

More Putney Families

Other friends at Putney were the Parkers, who lived in the Upper Richmond Road.

They once lived at Waihao Downs and Christchurch, N.Z. but came to Putney about the same time we did. Mr Parker was a brother of Mrs Archibald Smith, whose son Arthur married my first cousin Gertrude. The Parkers had two sons, James and Pat, who both went into the Navy, and three daughters Cecily, Ruth and Mary. Ruth was my age, Cecily was Esmé's age.

The Oates were another family, two sons and two daughters, Laurence and Bryan, and Lilian and Violet. Their father was a well known explorer. They moved to Gestingthorpe Hall in Essex, but I forget when. Laurence, of course, is one of England's great heroes. Mr Oates died abroad in 1896. Lilian married the famous singer Mr Frederic Ranalow who sang for <u>six years</u> in the Beggar's Opera. They travelled round the world with Melba in 1909 for their honeymoon and Lilian spent a few hours at Hiwiroa with us. (see Book II)

Lawrence Oates, 17 March 1880 – 16 March 1912

He was a brave soul. This was the end... It was blowing a blizzard. He said, 'I am just going outside and may be some time'. He went out into the blizzard and we have not seen him since.

The Drydens were older than us - they were Helen's and Esther's friends. Kate and I stayed with them in 1893 while Tom was packing up at Disraeli Road. Lady Dryden was a champion sneezer. I once counted seventeen sneezes! And Sir Arthur gardened in his long brick walled garden behind the house. They afterwards went to live at Canons Ashley, and I think all of them are dead now - they were a kind and cheerful family.

Mr and Mrs Olding had us all to Christmas dinner on Boxing Day and gave a children's party afterwards, so we always had <u>two</u> Christmas dinners. When we were little we stayed the night afterwards. Mrs Olding often had one of us to stay with her; she would drive over in a high dog cart and go home with a lucky child. I always stayed with her every year after I was grown up, and in 1912 Norton and George and Phyllis and Nanny King and I all stayed there. Mr Olding had died very suddenly in 1897. Dr Dawes told me the sad news and took me to see poor Mrs Olding the next afternoon. She had known Dr Dawes' family for years, and it was she who persuaded Father to send Kate and me to her school, so it was a grief to Dr Dawes too.

Musical evenings

Tom used to take Kate and me to musical parties given by Mrs Hobart-Hampden, sister of Tom's great friend Miss Druitt. I think Mrs Hobart-Hampden lived in Kensington. She had an only child called Gertrude. The parties were an ordeal, as each child had to play or sing or recite, but after that was over we had a party tea, and then played games; 'Turn the Trencher' and 'Family Coach' etc. I had to play my fiddle. Kate would recite. She learnt the piano until she was fourteen, but her very thin fingers were not suitable for the piano. When she first began to learn she could hardly push the notes down. She had a few lessons on the violin with the idea that she could play the viola, but that was soon given up as she just squeaked on her little fiddle and walked about the house quite amused with the noise.

Best friend, her sister Kate

It is difficult to write about Kate, she was so very much my other half; we were dressed alike and did things together, but were not a bit alike in character. She was never shy, would always do 'the asking' in a shop, was never afraid of people, quite philosophical about things and never a cry baby like me. We looked alike in a photograph but had different colouring. She had rather a brown skin and dark hazel eyes and light brown wavy hair which fell in ringlets and curled round her face in the rain. The curls were cut off when she was three, but grew again when she was twelve. She was never very strong but was energetic. Helen adored her, and Tom called her 'Little Sweet'. Tom sometimes took me to see our cousins Sir Frank and Lady Marzials. He was a first cousin of Father's and Cousin Julia was his second wife. He was extremely good looking with courtly manners, and she was pretty and I expect a good deal younger. There was a grown up family and the two little girls that I went to see were younger than me. Ada was a dear little thing and called me Cuckoo because I sang her a kindergarten song about cuckoos, and the younger one was Phyllis Daphne. I went to her Christening. I have quite lost sight of them. Ada Marzials wrote the 'Land of Nursery Rhyme' children's books.

Uncle George and Aunt Carrie

In 1892 Uncle George and Aunt Carrie came into our lives. They lived at Henfold in Ceylon where Uncle George had a coffee plantation. When coffee failed disastrously in 1884 he was ruined too, but his half-brother Edward Beck lent him £50,000 and he started to grow tea instead.

Rev Blomfield Jackson Married Bessie Beck in 1867 and had four children. If Edward Beck is George's half brother, who was his mother? And who was George's? Maud says his mother was called Susanna and he had brothers and sisters called Marcus, John, Ellen and Edith.

He must be the George who appears in the following list as an owner of Henfold tea plantation in Ceylon.

OWNERS OF HENFOLD

Admiral Sir Thomas Jackson	1929 - 1930
Heirs of late George Beck	1928 - 1928
Mrs. George Beck	1925 - 1927
Trustees of the late Geor...	1920 - 1921
George Beck	1917 - 1917
G. Beck.	1904 - 1914

That was the beginning of Ceylon tea. He and Aunt Carrie stayed for eight years in Ceylon, until the tea was beginning to pay. They came back to England in 1892 and we saw them constantly and adored them. I always felt 'good' with Aunt Carrie; she never rubbed one up the wrong way like Aunt Nora who was sometimes in charge of us at Putney. Uncle George believed in chocolates and treats for children and a bag of chocolates always came with him or Aunt Carrie. She wore such pretty clothes too and was always bright and happy. We knew Uncle George's relations well, they lived in an old house at Isleworth - we called his Mother Aunt Susanna although she was our cousin's aunt, not ours. Uncle George's brothers Marcus and John lived there and his sisters Ellen and Edith. They all used to come and see us at Putney. Marcus was a clever surgeon and was, I think, one of Mother's doctors. John was one of the trustees of Mother's property. Ellen and Edith were short and clever and rather bossy, and had bulldogs. There was one bulldog called Daisy, a huge white creature that was rather overpowering to a child. She always seemed to have a large pink tongue hanging out of her mouth! Aunt Susanna dressed in lovely white frills and white shawls, and sat in a low ceilinged drawing room looking on to the lawn of the big garden. There was another brother Roger who lived at The Mumbles, whom I do not remember, and the half brother Edward, the eldest of them all, lived close by at Isleworth. They were all Quakers, and all original and clever.

More Putney friends

Other friends at Putney were Colonel and Mrs Durnford who afterwards moved to Weybridge. Colonel Durnford was at the War Office when Father was there, and when I was five I made him a pincushion and gave it to him saying 'This is in case your things come down at the War Office'. Needless to say I never heard the end of this strange remark.

The churches at Putney and Fulham

The Vicar of Putney was Mr Henley, and his son was one of the Curates. We went to the Parish Church, St. Mary's, by the river. There was a gallery at the west end which had a clock on it, but we were not supposed to turn round in church and see what the time was. The services used to seem very long to us. We always had Matins and the Litany and the Ante-Communion Service. Kate and I did not like going to church, but we knew that Tem and Helen were 'good churchwomen'. We used to go to the Children's services at Fulham sometimes, and that was enjoyed.

My memories of Fulham are of a bright church, not dark like St. Mary's.

All saints Fulham 1755 – painting by Joseph Nicholls with kind permission of John Bennett fine paintings.

We used to sit behind two sturdy little wide boys in dark tweed suits. They were the sons of the Bishop of London, Dr Temple, who lived at Fulham Palace, and one of them is now Archbishop of York. I can remember the Bishop too; he had a very large <u>square</u> head. Fulham had flower services once a year, when every child took flowers or a plant to church, which were sent to Children's Hospitals. This service was a great treat. I was not at all a religious child and even disliked the Scripture lessons at school which were very dry. But I cannot have been quite void of religion, for when I was told not to say 'God bless Mother' in my prayers after Mother's death, I can remember thinking 'You are quite wrong, I ought to pray for Mother'. I was sitting on someone's lap; I think it was Tem's lap. I expect she and the others found my prayer rather trying. We used to have horrible English grammar lessons at the College and be given passages of 'Paradise Lost' to analyse. (This dreadful custom was still going on when I went to school at Weybridge).

The school examiner

One day Mr I. Gollancz came to examine the school. We were told he was a genius and trembled accordingly. I was about ten. He wore a bright magenta tie. The afternoon ordeal was English Grammar for all the school. I was sitting in front and his first question was to me 'Do you like Grammar?' 'No I <u>don't</u>'. I said. He smiled, and there were no more questions, but he talked to us about words and about English. I was too young to understand him, except that Grammar had suddenly become interesting. We also had to read Paradise Lost for Literature but it was never made clear to me that it was all Milton's imagination. I looked in the Old Testament to find Paradise Lost and when it could not be found thought it was because I was too stupid to look in the right place. I still think Milton's ideas about God and Heaven quite horrible and not fit for a young child to read. I believed in prayer, especially prayer to help one out of a difficulty, but was certainly not a religious child or a good child. I was listening the other day to a radio sermon by a priest about the 'showers of blessings' that God gives us, and certainly all my life I have been showered with blessings. But in the Putney day I did not realize this. I disliked the school and all the driving and hammering of facts there, and I disliked Putney and the smuts of London, and the constant winter fogs, and I was over-sensitive and touchy about lots of things. And yet, although we were badly off, there was always enough to eat and Tem surrounded us with kindness, and gave us all the clothes and treats that were possible, and Aunt Bessy and Mrs Olding and many friends were very kind to us.

Life with Nanny Tem

We did no housework. There was always a cook and a housemaid, and all the washing except our black stockings, was sent away to be washed. The nurse Blanche left in 1886 when I was six, I suppose so as to save expense, and Tem took entire charge of Kate and me then and we always slept in her room. When Helen came back from France in 1887 she must have led a dull life. She used to get up very late and her breakfast would be left for her at the end of the dining room table. She read a great deal and helped Tem with the mending, and when Tem went away for a holiday she did the housekeeping and was very strict with us. As long as the elder ones were at home there was a rule that we three youngest ones should not speak at meals. It was called the 'Bibs On' rule and we were not allowed to talk until we had finished and the feeders were taken off. For years and years I found it very difficult to talk at mealtimes.

A public event and the frozen Thames

The first public event that I can remember is the death of General Gordon. I can remember people talking about it. They must have told me about the desert, for I wondered why, if he was in a sandy place, he did not row away in a boat. Sand meant seashore to me. The death of the Duke of Clarence is remembered because Mrs Olding and Tem took me to the Memorial Service in the Chapel Royal at Hampton Court, and we walked across the frozen Thames. The Chapel was draped in black and Tem said afterwards that I was the only person not in black - I wore the usual navy blue coat and frock.

(Between 1600 and 1814, it was not uncommon for the River Thames to freeze over for up to two months at a time. There were two main reasons for this; the first was that Britain (and the entire Northern Hemisphere) was locked in what is now known as the 'Little Ice Age'. The other catalyst was the medieval London Bridge and its piers, and specifically how closely spaced together they were. During winter, pieces of ice would get lodged between the piers and effectively dam up the river, meaning it was easier for it to freeze.)

Family Changes. Father comes home and gets married to Marion Crane

In the end of 1892 the family changes began. Harold left and we all wept our hearts out. Father came back in October 1892, got engaged to Miss Marion Crane (whom he met at Trinidad or Barbados) and was married on November 5th in London and a few days later left for Jamaica, where he was appointed Commodore of the Royal Navy Dockyard. For the next three years he lived at Admiralty House Jamaica. Helen and Esther went with him to Jamaica, and the year before Harold left home for good too, as a Midshipman in the flagship of the North American and West Indian Squadron. Tom went to the same squadron in 1893 I think it was - so half our family was in the West Indies.

Father goes back to Port Royal Jamaica

*This is a view of Port Royal about 1890, showing the church and town, looking west towards the entrance to Kingston Harbour. The town's heyday was in the seventeenth century when it served as headquarters for the buccaneers who pillaged the Spanish Main, but all that came to an end with the disastrous earthquake of 1692, when more than half of the town was swallowed up by the sea. What remained was a small fishing village with a naval station and dockyard, but even that would pass away. By 1881 the population was 1205, exclusive of shipping. According to Michael Pawson and David Buisseret in their book, **Port Royal, Jamaica**(1975)*

Helen and Esther went with him and took with them many new clothes, including quantities of underclothes made of white nun's veiling. I can remember so well seeing them made in Tem's studio, but why tickly nun's veiling for the material I cannot imagine. It must have been someone's 'good advice'.

Helen was a bridesmaid at Father's wedding and looked very pretty in deep cream silk trimmed with gold silk, and gold coloured feathers in her cream hat. She had thick straight black hair and her eyelashes were so dark that they made her eyes look black, although they were really a dark blue grey. Esther wore one of her new dresses, a light blue and white patterned foulard. Tem had a pretty new dress too, a soft blue with narrow bands of mink at neck and wrists. We three had blue dresses too, rather the same shade, and pale grey felt hats trimmed with the same blue. I can remember Nanette at the reception afterwards, and wondering who the little girl was. She was Nanette Murray and her uncle, Captain Charles Farquharson, was married to a sister of my new step-mother. They all left for Jamaica a few days later, and we were taken to Waterloo Station to see them off.

Poor Kate broke down after the train left and was taken home by Tem, but Esmé and I went to school where, of course, we were fiercely greeted with enquiries as to why we were late. Esmé said 'We have been to Waterloo to see Father off' and then she got a bit weepy and we were both forgiven the sin of coming late.

How we dressed

The following spring Esmé was Confirmed in St. Mary's Church, and we saw the service from the gallery. And when we were about twelve or so Kate and I suddenly began to grow. Esmé had always seemed so tall and strong and so much older, but now we were catching her up. Kate once boasted that she had bigger hands, bigger feet and a bigger waist than I! I can remember the grownups laughing about this and wondering what the joke was. But Kate and I still shared the same clothes and Tem used to mark our underclothes M.K.J. because they did for either of us. We were dressed alike for many years. We always wore navy serge in the winter, made with yokes, bishop's sleeves gathered at the wrists and gathers at the waist. There was a pocket in the seam of the skirt. At neck and wrists were tuckers - frilled pieces of embroidery which were tacked in every week. We did not always wear them in our cuffs as they got so dirty at school. At school we always wore plain aprons made of brown Holland. At home we wore white pinafores. Frocks were made with tucks which were let down as you grew. In the summer we had print dresses. Best frocks were handed down. There was a black velvet frock worn with a pale silk sash of pale 'Roman' stripes in which I fancied myself. And Tem made me yellow cashmere from some stuff she found among Mother's things, which was afterwards dyed peacock blue. We wore plain straw sailor hats, real sailor-shaped in the summer, and when we were little we wore sunbonnets, which we hated because the starched strings were scratchy and made funny sounds in your ears. Mother had taken great care of her children's feet, and our boots and shoes were made to measure by Mr. Harvey (I think that was the name) of Plymouth. He still made for us when we moved to Putney and the outline of our feet was drawn on paper and very tickly it was. We wore button boots and plain strap shoes. Owing to Mother's care and Tem's continuing it we all had straight feet and no cramped toes.

Reading books

I loved reading, and read every book I could find. We all belonged to the Free Library which was close to our house. I liked to kneel or crouch on the floor and cover up my ears from the family noises and read by the hour. Favourites were Old *Punches* and *Illustrated London News* which taught me modern history from 1840 on, *'Extraordinary Popular Delusions'* - Norton had a copy of this book too - *Kane's Arctic Explorations* and a series of historical stories by Emily S. Holt, also the What *Katy Did books* and Miss Alcott's. But I would read anything, *The Nineteenth*

Century and Quarterly Magazines! Unabridged. *Gulliver's Travels* and *Robinson Crusoe* and perhaps favourite of all was *Masterman Ready* and later I loved *King Solomon's Mines.* Kate and I liked a book called *'Notable Shipwrecks'* which we pronounced Not Able Shipwrecks! No, I think on second thoughts that *Cranford* was my favourite. I read it several times from the age of nine. Tem used to read out loud to us and when she read Pickwick we would roll about on the floor with laughter. The only books she advised me not to read were *Trilby* and *Oliver Twist.* When I was grown up of course I read them, and am thankful that I had not done so before, for both books made me shudder.

Maud's thirteenth birthday and a visit to see Shakespeare

At Easter 1893 I had my thirteenth birthday. Uncle George and Aunt Carrie had taken a small house on the hills near Godalming and asked Tem and Kate and me to stay with them. We went on Good Friday and returned on Monday evening. It was a perfect spring, and to be in the country in the springtime was pure joy to us - we saw Celandines for the first time and Crown Imperials - it was sunny and mild all the time and we went for drives in an open landau, and I was given a half crown wrapped up in a big parcel for a birthday present.

Later that year Aunt Carrie gave me another great treat. She took me to see 'The Merchant of Venice' acted by Sir Henry Irving and Ellen Terry. I knew the play almost by heart so could enjoy it all. It was not the first time I had been to Shakespeare at the Lyceum Theatre for a year or two before Esmé and I went with our form at school to see 'Much Ado About Nothing'. We sat in the front row of the upper circle. Miss Redpath our headmistress took us, and had read and almost acted the play with us beforehand. Ellen Terry wore a stiff brocade dress and was entrancing, but I can remember thinking that Irving was not a beautiful enough lover for her. The Claudio was far handsomer! But Miss Redpath thought him perfect. She taught us English Literature very well for she was enthusiastic, so from the first we enjoyed Caedmon and Chaucer and then she led us on to Shakespeare.

Mumps

That summer of 1893 Kate had suppressed mumps, and three weeks later poor Tem had very swollen mumps so we did not go to school and missed all the examinations of our last term. We romped about the house and garden and did what we liked for nobody came near us except the Drydens. Tom had leave that summer and took photographs of us playing 'Sevens' in the garden and allowed me to watch him developing in one of the cellars.

Off to Germany. The beginning of years of travel

Tem took Esmé, Kate and me to Kassel in Germany in October 1893, where we stayed until 1895, and that was the beginning of several years of travelling for us. We crossed the Channel from Dover to Ostend and once more I enjoyed the 'uppity-down feeling' which I loved when going to and from the Isle of Wright. When we got to Ostend and were abroad at last we were very excited. We left at once for Cologne, and stared out of the windows at Belgium until it got dark. When we

Cologne Cathedral

reached Herbesthal at the frontier we had to leave the train and go through the Customs, then back to the train, and arrived at Cologne at 11 p.m. We went at once to the Hotel Domerhof close to the railway station and straight to bed - our first night in German beds which were so different to English ones. In the morning we had breakfast of coffee and rolls in the dining room. It had many windows looking on to the Platz. Tem had often been to Germany and could speak just enough German to get all she wanted and to understand more or less what was said. She used to go to Volkershausen, on the river Werra, to stay with the Baroness Von Und Zu Gilsa and teach her younger daughter, Countess Kathy, painting.

The Baroness was English, Miss Dunbar-Masson, and the Baron was Austrian I think, and had been an official at the Viennese Court. I think he was Chamberlain. To go back to Cologne, it was a grey day but not raining. After breakfast we went to the Cathedral, the beautiful Kolner Dom. We noticed the great height, and the lovely pillars which look almost like groups of slender trees, the roof being their branches. We were shown the Treasury which I remember was brightly lit and full of gold holy vessels bright with jewels. In the centre was a wonderful gold reliquary in which are the bones of the Three Wise Men. The priest opened a small door in the Reliquary for us to look inside.

We must have spent some time in the Cathedral for that is all that we saw of Cologne except the Rhine and the Rhine bridge. We left after lunch by train for Kassel where we were to live. Once more we stared out of the windows and were amused to see Halt at every level crossing - it looked an English word to us and we thought it funny. When we got to Kassel we went to the Kaiser Fredrick Wilhelm Hotel where we stayed for a week or two while Tem found a boarding house for us

The hotel was great fun, the German food and table d'hote, the kind Portiere at the front door who spoke English. I ate blue eel one day - but never again! The service at table was slow, and I started my bad habit of nibbling bread between the courses to pass the time. We had been trained <u>not</u> to speak at mealtimes remember.

Exploring Kassel

It was great fun exploring Kassel, seeing the sights, looking at shop windows and looking at the totally different dresses of the people. Kassel was the capital of Hessen - Kassel which had been annexed by Prussia in 1866. The new town is built on high rocky ground above the River Fulda - a swift clean river. The old town was built on the river, and there was a bridge leading to the chief part of the old town. This was very pretty, high old red roofed houses and very narrow streets, like a fairy story old German town. On one house there was a Memorial Plaque to an old woman who had told the brothers Grimm the local fairy stories. They are known to English people for the stories, but were very learned men and renowned for their studies. Kassel was famous for other things - the largest Platz in Germany, just like a huge barrack square surrounded by rather dingy looking old palaces and buildings; a splendid picture gallery full of treasures, including seventeen Rembrandts and a collection of Wouvermans; an academy of painting where at that time Herr Knackfuss was director. He was the artist who helped the Kaiser paint his picture of the Yellow Peril. Some said he did all the painting! The ancient Nibelungenlied was treasured there too; it is a German epic poem about Siegfried. When we studied a few lines of it at a Literature lesson, our master was interested to notice that I could read it, or rather, guess at reading the old German which looked rather like Caedmon Saxon English. Then there was the boys' Grammar School where the Kaiser had been sent as a boy. Three miles from Kassel is the palace of Wilhelmshöhe built in the eighteenth century when every reigning king or prince wanted a Versailles - I like Wilhelmshöhe much better than Versilles! There seemed to be a great many places about Kassel, from the times when it was a capital with its own court. There was a Court Theatre.

When we went to Kassel it was one of the three healthiest towns of Germany, the others being Dresden and Weimar. Tem chose Kassel, as Dresden had so many English people living there and Weimar she thought would be too much of the 'small-town'. We liked Kassel, it seemed so clean and bright after London, and many of the streets had avenues of trees. We lived in the Avenue leading to Wilhelmshaven - No.8 Wilhelmshöhe Allee. The two top floors were a pension, or boarding house, kept by a German lady, Frau Von Buttlar. Her husband had been in the Army and was dead. Her maiden name was Von Reiche, and so, although she was badly off and kept a small boarding house, she belonged to Court circles. One daughter was grown up and lived at home, and the two younger children were both at State schools for the orphans of officers, and only came home once a year. The boy was only about ten, and wore an army uniform. Frau Von Buttlar was short and stout, very plainly dressed, with straight dark hair, very outspoken and worked very hard. She was kind to us, but I think life had been a struggle to her and she never seemed to have any religion. We knew that Tem did not think she was a 'lady', but then Tem never shouted at servants, nor cleaned up her plate with a piece of bread, and was always being shocked by various bits of strange behaviour. On the other hand Frau Von Buttlar was a clever woman, spoke excellent English and was a practical housewife. I went with her one day to the meat market and saw her handling the raw meat and choosing the pieces she wanted and stupid me thought it was horrid! We had two bedrooms and a sittingroom on the lower floor of the two flats. The sittingroom was warmed by a large stove, and during the winter months double windows were fitted, which kept out the frost. The winters that we spent in Germany were very severe ones, like the 1939-40 winter in England, and the cold was intense from Christmas to the end of April, so that I always think of a German winter as a very snowy affair. But I cannot remember being cold in the house, and did not have chilblains or a cold in my head while we were there.

Freezing winter

Out of doors when the wind blew from Russia as we called it, the cold was really rather unbearable. The country was covered with thick snow. Paths were made through the snow in the streets by piling snow at the side over the gutters - long icicles hung from the roofs and from the branches of the trees in the avenues. The river froze and there was skating on a lake near the river. On Sundays the band played on the lake and everyone skated. We got tired of skating as the months went by and did not bother to go. Wheels were taken off the carts and runners put on instead. Once we went for a sleigh ride in the country, but the cold was so intense that it was nice to get home. One needs fur coats and caps for that sort of icy weather. Sometimes, if we came in very cold, Tem would give us Gluhwein, which is claret and hot water and sugar and bay leaves, and sometimes when we started out she would take us to a nearby confectioner's and order hot chocolate for us - but these were rare treats. We wore our ordinary English winter clothes plus galoshes which kept one's feet dry. In April came the thaw, and that was the worst part for it was not safe to walk along the paths until men had shovelled the snow off the roofs and the icicles had fallen from trees and houses, and it was also extremely slippery and felt so damp and horrid. Suddenly the thaw was over, the sun was hot, flowers everywhere and everything looked lovely. We never had burst pipes, for in the autumn all outside taps and pipes were covered up, and the water mains were buried deeply and houses kept warm with stoves. Rose trees were bent over and piles of fir branches put on top and this kept them from harm.

To Fräulein Henser's school

We went to a private school kept by Fräulein Henser. It was called a Höhere Töchterschule, or high-daughters'-school, otherwise, in old fashioned English, a school for the daughters of gentlemen. It was both a boarding and day school and we were day girls. There were over 200 girls, and the school was in a large high red brick house standing in a small asphalt yard on a hilly street. There were large windows on all sides of the house and the bigger school rooms looked out on two sides and so were bright and well lighted. Windows were closed during lessons and the rooms got very stuffy and smelly. I was always in one of the ground floor rooms and only went upstairs for dancing and for private literature lessons. Kate too was on the ground floor. At first Esmé and I were in the same class, but after a time she was moved to a senior girls' class called the Selects, I think composed of girls who had been Confirmed but who still took a few classes. Kate and I thought they never did anything much! The lowest class was the 10th and the top class was the 1st. There were about thirty girls in our classes. Esmé was 15½ years old I was 13½ and Kate 12½ in our new school, which was such a complete change from the College. At first we knew no German, or practically none, although Esmé and I had learnt a little at the College, where it must have been taught very badly as we were given Anderson's Fairy Tales in German to translate instead of learning some easy sentences. The German characters puzzled me and the print was very small, so I really knew no German at all.

At Fräulein Henser's school we were given a month's grace, and after that had to do all the preparation and essays done by the rest of the class. That first term one of the young assistant teachers came in the afternoons to help us with our preparation. I remember that we taught her Counties of England game - in German of course - and how difficult she found the names of the English towns. We had to learn German and very soon understood it fairly well. The lessons would have been very easy if we had not been handicapped by the language. Everything seemed to go slowly; especially Arithmetic and we learnt no Algebra, Euclid or Latin, nor Ancient History. A great deal of time was taken in writing everything out in copper plate German handwriting, and this of course, though tedious, did not employ our brains. We had to be at school at 8 a.m. Middle Europe Time which meant 7.40 by the sun. We stayed at school until 1p.m. and then walked home which took twenty minutes, and midday dinner was at 1.30p.m. We did all our preparation at home and were supposed to spend four hours over it. We had practising to do and music lessons to go to, so it was a busy afternoon, although one could manage with less than four hours preparation, and we often cut this time down considerably. Esmé and Kate had piano lessons and I had violin lessons from the same master, Herr Heinemann, who was a pupil of Spohr. Spohr had lived in Kassel and there was a copper statue of him which had turned very green. I expect he was melted down in the 1914-18 War. Herr Heinemann was a kindly old man, and I liked my lessons. It was not the fashion for girls to play the violin; I was the only one in our school. We all enjoyed the music at Kassel, Military bands and orchestras and operas. The best operas were always given on Sundays, and Tem drew the line at going to the theatre on Sundays so we did not hear them. Tem was never strict about Sunday doings but taught us never to offend other people's feelings on that day. We did not play games in the little garden on Sunday at Putney for fear of annoying the neighbours. But all quiet amusements and reading and sewing went on - and we were not made to read 'Sunday books'. When we were in Germany Sunday was often the only day when there was time to do one's mending. We were brought up to go to church on Sunday and to rest from lessons and to be happily amused. We never had any idea of the so called 'English Sunday' until we went to boarding school in 1896. We went to School on Saturday too, but often managed to give ourselves a half holiday on Saturday and go for long walks in the town in the winter, and to Wilhelmshöhe and into the country in the summer, and we went for walks on Sundays too. There was a little English Church and a resident Chaplain, Mr Thomas, who was married so we were not cut off from Church and always went to church at least once every Sunday. There were a handful of resident English people, and a few American and English visitors in the summer time. The English were all 'grown-ups' and I cannot remember much about them. We were always with German people.

We had to be at school before 8 a.m., hang up coats and hats in our schoolroom (there was no cloakroom) and put galoshes on the floor under our peg. At 8, the sliding doors were pushed back into the adjoining room and the whole school marched into our room, followed by Herr Pfarrer Fuchs (Mr Parson Fox) who conducted prayers. We slowly sang one verse of a hymn, Pfarrer Fuchs said a very short prayer, then we slowly sang what was called Die Guade (The Grace of Our Lord etc.) and that was all. Then lessons began, and we had five periods during the morning. Once a week 'drawing' took two hours and once a week needle work took two hours, otherwise each lesson lasted an hour. About eleven we had a short break, windows were opened, and if fine everyone rushed into the yard and ate something. We always took a crusty roll with us, with a bit of butter inside. Breakfast was never ready before we left home and the rolls arrived just as we left so we used to seize one and dab in the butter, and put it in a coat pocket. It never seemed to hurt us not having breakfast. We had a class mistress to teach us, a Mademoiselle for French, other mistresses for needlework and drawing, and masters for arithmetic, a very infantile kind of science, physical geography and German literature and essays. German history I found extremely dull although I was a history lover, lists of kings and dukes and dates and wars. French was difficult as one had to translate from German into French, the other girls once put me into Coventry because I did not cheat at French. It was mostly grammar-book translations of sentences, and the girls thought it clever to have the open book on their knees while we translated in class. They had quite different ideas about honour and also about cleanliness, but I had lots of friends among them. They only had a bath once a month and sometimes not so often, so the room used to get dreadfully stuffy. They looked tidy and everyone had one or two neat pigtails. We were taught to write very neatly in German handwriting, although most of our teachers' writing was bad. Although it was a private school the teachers had to be Government trained, and our timetables, which were pinned up on the wall, bore a Government stamp marked Berlin. We were taught needlework very well. It seemed that German mothers left this subject to the schools and we found that we were 'ahead of our class mates'. The first year I made a sampler out of a piece of linen, a sampler of plain needlework. All stitches were worked by the thread, and we were taught all kinds of stitches and seams. Except for a seam called Rollnad and for hemstitching, I knew all the stitches. The next year we had to make enormous chemises with short sleeves out of thick cream linen. Tem then managed to arrange for me to be excused from sewing class, and I turned my half-made chemise into tablecloths and embroidered them, much to the amusement of the needlework mistress. The next year my class was taught to darn, which was done by the thread over a piece of black American cloth. In Kate's class they were taught to knit stockings and I wish I had learnt this, for it turned Kate into such a good knitter she could knit anything and I have often seen her knitting while walking in the country, with the ball of wool tucked inside her blouse. Tem first taught me fancywork (embroidery) when I was nine, and while we were in Germany she encouraged me at this, and I made an embroidered sideboard cloth for Helen for a wedding present in 1894. We should think it very funny now, but it was fashionable then. I did every stitch myself and was annoyed when someone wrote to Tem after the wedding that it was easy to see that Tem had done most of the work. Another enjoyable lesson was class singing; we learnt the old German songs and hymns. I had a contralto voice and enjoyed singing seconds or thirds.

Geography lessons were rather a joke, especially when we were taught the geography of England –'England is divided into five sheers (sic), called Essex, Wessex, Kent, Northumberland and Cornwall'. This was in the book! And I was forced to repeat it by Fräulein, who also insisted on my pronouncing Iona as Jonah. Tem was so amused at our Geography book dating from the Heptarchy. I was in the English class for one term, but after that Tem once more arranged for me to be excused for it was a waste of time. It was not easy, as every girl was supposed to do every lesson. However, Fräulein Henser consented and I was allowed to have private German literature and composition lessons during the needlework and English lessons. Fräulein Martin taught the English and we had to learn a little rhyme beginning 'The bird sings sweetly on the bough' and I was told to say it - but at the end of the first line was stopped and corrected 'The bird zings sweetly on the Baw' being the correct accent.

Scripture was called Religion and was taught by Herr Pfarrer Fuchs. We had a small book of Bible stories but we were not allowed to have Bibles. One day some of the girls clustered round me and said they had heard that English people had Bibles and would I tell them all the disgusting things they were not allowed to read.

This was not even understood by me and I was horrified. There was a Catechism beginning 'Bist du ein Christ? Ja' (Art thou a Christian? Yes.) But Pfarrer Fuchs did not insist on my learning it. He once asked me who the first Man was, and without thinking I said I did not know, and he burst into a storm of scolding about the evil influence of Darwin. Of course I had never heard of Darwin! One Catechism had Ten Commandments and another only had nine according to Lutheran or Reformed, but I forget which was which. Kate amused Tem by coming home one day and saying she was sick of Luther, in her form they had nothing but Luther for months. The Reformed Church was the fashionable one at Kassel. Fräulein Selma Zeidler who was my class mistress during my last year told me that a long time ago there were such quarrels between the Lutherans and Reformers that it was tried to unite them in an United Church - but this only made a third church. She came from Berlin and belonged to the United Church, but this was a secret as she would not dare say so at Kassel. Living as we did with people who did not go to church nor say prayers, and who had never heard of 'grace' and talked of Confirmation as a coming out ceremony and party, is it any wonder that Tem used to tell our German friends that they were heathen? Luther was an important hero in History lessons too and one had to learn a great deal about the religious wars. I found out by this time that Luther broke his vows as a monk and married a nun, and this to me was just a man who broke his promises, and yet he was held up by our teachers as a great man.

We were taught dancing by a stoutish middle aged lady who was chief of the ballet and a good teacher. I think dancing was an extra. She was so different to charming graceful Madame de Tenionier, who taught dancing at the College, and made one long to be graceful and walk into a room like a queen. She used to walk around the room smiling and bowing to us while we all bowed and curtseyed. Once a week we walked in a crocodile to a gymnasium and amused ourselves on parallel bars and ladders and all the usual equipment. We wore our ordinary school clothes but we did not mind showing white drawers and petticoats and, funnily enough, I can't remember clothes getting in the way. Occasionally the gym mistress made us play a dreadful game of throwing a football to each other, it was dull because most of the girls could not catch, the football was a clumsy thing and there was no meaning in it all, it just went on until we were told to stop.

Our class mistress taught us free hand drawing, elaborate scrolls and leaves. It was difficult to make the right hand pattern match the left hand one. Herr Doktor Wechzel taught us arithmetic and science. We learnt the rule of three all the time I was at school. At the Tuesday lesson he set the sum (only one) on the blackboard and you made your rough copy, and on Friday you brought him the same sum beautifully written out in an exercise book of plain paper, with a neat little frame ruled round the sum. Doktor Wechzel had a violent temper. When Elsa von Brozowski, the prize naughty girl of the class, had a little mirror and made sun reflections dance about the blackboard, he was so furious that he picked up a chair and smashed it to pieces.

I started at school in class 5 and as soon as my German was better was moved into class 4 where Fräulein Martin was in charge. She had a fierce temper and frightened me. I used to comfort myself by thinking she would not dare to murder us. I must have been a dull pupil, often in a brown study, for the lessons as a rule just jogged on, there was none of the rush or enthusiasm of an English school. When we moved into class 3 under Fräulein Zeidler school life was much pleasanter. She had a gentle voice and gentle manners and was better educated and broader minded. She had been in England for five years as a governess and had not enjoyed being 'the governess' but had learnt to speak English perfectly. We had a good master for Literature and Composition, mostly the latter, Herr Doktor Zimmermann, a small fiery man with a red moustache whom we treated with respect. He once gave me a 'Praise' for an essay 'very good for a foreigner' being his remark, but before being allowed to have the 'Praise' I had to be interviewed by the Headmistress, class mistress and himself to assure them that I had not been helped. They were so used to cheating!

We did not have marks or prizes, but for any very good work you got Praise (Lob) and for bad work a Tadel or Blame - untidiness, laziness, forgetting to write out mistakes etc., earned you a bad mark and four bad marks equalled one Tadel. This was written on a piece of paper and you had to take it home with you and give it to your Mother. She gave you a whipping and when your father came home in the evening he gave you another whipping. When a girl received a Tadel there were floods of tears, and her friends would beg and beg the master or mistress to let her off, saying Bitte, Bitte, Bitte over and over again. The scene completely stopped the lesson. Kate wanted to know what Tem would do if she got a Tadel, so for four weeks running she did not write out her French spelling mistakes, got four bad marks and a Tadel which she proudly took home to poor Tem, who could only laugh and say 'You naughty child'.

One thing I never got used to at school was the swearing. Ach Du lieber Herr Gott! Ach Gott! Ach Du lieber Herr Jesu! And Gott said very quickly and often so that it sounded like Gottergottergott were heard every day. I do not think anyone realized how dreadful it was.

I have enlarged about our German lessons because so often one hears about the marvellous education in Germany. When we were there very little intellectual work was expected of girls, but boys were worked very hard and had very long hours. We learnt German which was why we were there, and it was very good for us to live with foreigners and get broader minded. Schools were used for propaganda. One day we were shown a diagram to scale of the English and German Navies. In 1894 the German Navy was small and the Kaiser wanted one larger if possible than England's. Just as the Nazis do, he started to influence the minds of the adolescents. Of course all the girls groaned that it wasn't fair of England, The same thing went on about the British Empire. England had too many Colonies and it was not fair. No German could remember that while English sailors were moving about the world and making discoveries and haphazardly almost collecting Colonies, Germany was a collection of little kingdoms and dukedoms, often at war with each other and not in the least interested in the sea. We were also told about the wickedness of England 'owning' India and shown a picture of a tiger which was England clawing at a map of India (It <u>was</u> a tiger not a lion). All this was going on in a school for young ladies twenty years before the Great War of 1914 began.

Anti-Semitism

They were horrid to the Jews and seemed to be so jealous of them. When I had my fourteenth birthday I asked a few of my school friends to coffee (coffee not tea in Germany). A day or two later when I got to school I was ordered to go to the Head-mistress' room. She asked me if it were true that I had had a certain girl to my birthday party. This was a very pretty fair girl with lovely curly golden hair and nice manners and always well dressed. She was always present at prayers and "Religious" lessons and one only vaguely remembered that she was of Jewish family. We heard afterwards that the grandparents were Jews, the parents were nothing and the children were to choose their religion when the time came for Confirmation. One of my other guests had told her Mother that I had asked a Jewess to my party, and this Mother complained to Fräulein Henser of the insult. Fräulein Henser soon understood that we did not know that Germans do not mix socially with Jews, and I was foreign! Someone was staying at Frau Von Buttlar's once who was very bitter about Jews, and never entered one of their shops. As nearly all the good shops in Kassel belonged to Jews she could only go to the third rate ones. We often heard envious remarks about Jews having all the money and owning the newspapers etc. They were not allowed to go to the Court parties when the Kaiser's sister was staying in Kassel. By the way we were told that she smoked all the time at evening parties and receptions.

Swimming in the summer

When the summer came the swimming baths in the river were opened, and we had season tickets and went as often as possible. We had learnt to swim at the very good swimming baths at Putney and all could swim well, Kate being far the best. The German baths were great fun, with a water shoot, and the swift river water always passing through. The baths were in the river, built of poles which kept out all leaves and rubbish. Skating and swimming were the only games we could have, but Tem believed in fresh air and long walks for us and we got exercise that way. There were two or three tennis courts in the Gardens, where we used to see officers playing, often in uniform. They always wore uniform with stiff high collars, and dangling swords. The Kaiser allowed them to play tennis in flannels but they were not allowed to move off the court except in uniform. Officers and soldiers were everywhere,

Kassel being a great military centre. The officers took precedence over everyone and walked as if the world was theirs. We thought their manners in the street were rude, if they were walking three or four abreast everyone else had to get out of their way. The policemen wore long great coats and swords too, the swords reaching the ground. They were the opposite of London policemen and seemed to be there to boss you, not to help.

Clothing described

The peasants in the country near Kassel wore their special dress, but as they were poor it was not very gay. The married women dragged their hair to the top of their heads and wore a little black cap on it to hide the bun. The cap was just like a round box. The older women wore a high pointed black headdress - which was much more becoming. Tem painted one of these women and it was one of her most successful portraits. She used to work under Herr Knackfuss at the Academy while we were at school. The peasants wore many short petticoats and cross over shawls. People who could afford nurses for their babies dressed the girls in the correct costume of the country, many petticoats reaching to just below the knee, almost of ballet dress fullness, thick white woollen stockings, gay colours, ribbons hanging from some of the headdresses - the ribbons were not as beautiful as we saw the Paris 'bonnes'
wearing when we lived in Paris - and a wide ribbon supporting the little mattress on which the baby was carried. This mattress was covered with a kind of pillowcase, embroidered and trimmed with lace, and the baby slipped in with only its head showing. It must have been comfortable for the baby, and the ribbon took some of the weight from the nurses' arms. The poorer women of the town were all very neat. One never saw the rags and dirty skirts dragging in the mud that made one so unhappy in London. They all wore dresses of navy, dark blue and yellow print in small patterns, cotton dresses and cotton aprons and short enough not to get the hems dirty. The maids wore the same sort of dress.

Tem teaches about the poor

Tem used to take us to see her poor people in her district in London and so did Mrs. Olding sometimes and we saw the misery of the street beggars, and little ragged boys with no shoes or stockings. Helen used to make us write out lists of how we would spend weekly wages of say £1 for a man, wife and five children. We were brought up to realize the great poverty around us and to help and give what we could. We three belonged to the Ministering Children's League which worked, among other things, for the Evelina Hospital for Sick Children. I have never forgotten those sad sights of poverty, but in Germany the people never looked so poor because they mended their clothes and were tidy. The people of the business and professional classes wore different clothes to English people, but it was just different fashions and materials. Both men and women got very fat in early middle age and had barrel figures.

Modes of transport

Of course there were no motors in those days, and there were not many carriages. We never saw the beautiful carriages and horses and powdered footmen that I remember in Hyde Park and also driving through Putney - high barouches with grand ladies inside holding parasols, coachmen on the box and two footmen behind, and everything, horses, harness and carriage shining and brilliant. At Kassel the only cabs were called Droschkes and the drivers wore many coats. The cab was a kind of Victoria. There was a steam tram from Kassel to Wilhelmshohe and a few horse trams. We used to go to Wilhelmshohe by the steam tram and then walk up the hundreds of steps to the statue of Hercules and to open country beyond, or through the woods to Wilhelmsthal where was a gem of a small Rococo palace. Sometimes we went a short way by train and walked back. The country was lovely and quite "unspoilt" and we enjoyed these walks.

The summer term came to an end at the beginning of July and Tem took us away for three months. The summer holidays only lasted a month and at the beginning of August there was another term which ended after two months for the Kartoffelferien - potato holidays - when children were supposed to help their parents dig the potatoes. There were no potatoes in Kassel for anyone to dig, but in Prussian governed countries everybody must do the same thing. We had heard that girls did very little work during August and September, the hottest months, and we should hardly miss anything if we stayed away, so Tem removed us for long holidays.

On Holiday in Switzerland

First we went to Volkershausen (see left) to stay with the Von-Gilsas.

Katie was at home, a delightful girl about twenty, who took charge of us and taught us to row on the Werra which flowed past the garden. We used to swim in it too and it was a struggle to get across in anything like a straight line for the current was so swift. We drove about with Katie in a pony cart and we all went out to tea at another Schloss. Katie's name was the Contessa Kathe Von und Zu Gilsa - The Von Gilsas and their friends all spoke English and seemed like the people we had known in England, but they were of high rank. The farmyard of the Schloss at Volkershausen joined the house, so from some of the upstairs windows one looked

38

on to the farmyard and animals and sheds - and a manure heap which was not our idea of a castle! There were weeding women in the garden which reminded us of one of Mrs Ewing's books, was it not in 'Mary's Meadow'? We were only at Volkershausen for a short time and went on to Frankfurt am Main by a slow and very hot train which reached there after dark.

Chateau- d'Oeux, Switzerland

We changed into the Basle train and travelled through Switzerland the next day, past Gruyere to Chateau-d'Oeux where we stayed for a few weeks. There I saw my first mountain, the Gumfluh, and knelt at my bedroom window and almost adored it. Chateau d'Oeux in1894 was just a village with a funny little hill in the middle on which perched the church and a scattering of other houses and boarding houses all built of wood and very simple. It is in a wide grassy valley with hills to climb on each side and the loveliest wild flowers and wild strawberries. We were very happy there and ran wild, and Kate and I used to swing on the hotel swing at every spare moment, especially after meals. I can remember the grown-ups astonishment at this, but we did not know what they meant. Swinging was a Joy, therefore swing as much as you can. It was fun too, meeting fresh people and speaking French Instead of German. I have many happy memories of Chateau D'Oeux. One is of a bank of campanulas growing wild, every variety of height, just a lovely garden of blues. Another is of scrambling up to a little natural rock garden on the slopes of the Gumfluh, a *jardin des plantes* the Swiss called it, and seeing cyclamen growing wild. And going to another village nearer Gruyère, called Rossinières, and trying to draw a picture of a Swiss house carved all over.

Maud's big sisters get married

It was in this year that our elder sisters were married and our stepsister was born. Esther was married in March to Captain Hugh Robert Evans RN, who was Captain of HMS *Urgent*, the guard ship at Port Royal, Jamaica. She was married in the Dockyard Chapel at Port Royal and I think the entire Jamaican world went to the wedding. Esther was twenty one in July that year and Hugh twice her age.

> *In 1911 Captain Hugh Robert Evans RN, retired, was residing at Belvoir. His family was recorded as: Esther Louisa wife; their children: Bertha Helen; Margaret Esther; Clara Joan; Douglas Frederick; Leslie Ernest; George D. They had two other sons not recorded in the 1911 records, Thomas Hugh born in 1895 and Robert Henry born in 1897. The staff at Belvoir were: Eliza Beatrice Holwill a general servant; Mary Ann James a nurse; May Penrose a servant and Susan Webster a servant. Captain Hugh Roberts was born at St Albans in 1853 and married Esther Louisa Jackson of Plymouth in 1894, they moved from Penzance to Belvoir in about 1902.*

Helen was then engaged to an Army subaltern, Clifford Coffin, who was in the Royal Engineers and had been stationed at Jamaica. He was transferred to Ireland, so Helen went back to England by herself and had a quiet wedding in August. She stayed with Uncle Blomfield and Aunt Bessy at Mecklenburgh Square and I think Uncle Blomfield married her. Helen was twenty-five when she married and Clifford a year younger. We could not be bridesmaids to Helen as we were abroad, but Clifford very kindly sent us each a bridesmaid present, the initials H and C in pearls on a gold tiepin brooch. The little stepsister Rose was born In Jamaica in October after we had got back to Kassel.

Clifford Coffin VC

Continued Travels in Switzerland and Health Matters

From Chateau-d'Oeux we moved to Le Sepey, a small village, not very interesting. From there we walked one day to Leysin which was then a village of brown wood cottages on a high ledge above the valleys, with a lovely view across to mountains on the other side of the Rhone valley. There were quantities of wild flowers everywhere and there were no consumptives there then. Violet Clark and her German governess had joined us at Chateau-d'Oeux, and Violet objected to Sepey as too quiet, so next we moved to Glion which is 1000 ft. above the Lake of Geneva and between Monteux and Caux. It was not quiet there, for there was so much to see and do and we made many excursions. I should like to see the Lake of Geneva again. It is so beautiful and the sunsets seen from Glion or from Lausanne were as lovely as the sunsets one sometimes sees in the Pacific before reaching Panama. Tem took us to see Lausanne, Vevey, Monteux, Caux, Chillon and Geneva - also across to St Guigolphe which is partly in France and partly in Switzerland. We learned Byron's poetry about the Lake and found Chillon very interesting. Vie had thought it just a touristy-show place, instead of which it thrills one like the Tower of London almost. Kate caught butterflies for her collection and Tem sketched in water colours. Kate had not been strong and the butterfly collection was an amusement for her, only I generally had to do the running about and she did the killing. I don't think Kate was ever really strong but her muscles were strong and she was energetic. She suffered from constipation and Tem had to take her to a German Specialist in Gottingen and he wanted to keep her in his hospital to study! She was always the leader of us two. She was never shy, and would take the tickets and do the asking in a shop, and talk to strangers ever since she was quite small. Esmé was the strong one and independent and liked to make her own friends. She hated to be what we called 'interfered with'. She too was not shy and made friends with strangers and always seemed to know all about everybody when we had only been a few hours in a place. She was very seldom ill. We all had chicken pox at Kassel, caught at school, and she and I had had measles, but otherwise I don't think I can remember her ever being ill. Kate was often away from school but not Esmé. I had a weak chest, and had inflammation of the lungs as a baby and again when I was five, and constantly got bronchitis in the winter. Both Harold and I were always catching colds, and I had fierce bilious attacks too, but on the whole was stronger than Kate.

Back to Germany

Our next move was back to Germany, stopping at Basle on the way to see the Museum, and then on to Freiburg near the Black Forest where we stayed for two weeks. It is a Cathedral town and has a University and many old houses. It was a charming old German town. The Cathedral has a spire which looks like stone lace. It was autumn now and all the trees were changing colour so we thought Black was the last name to call the beautiful forests. We went to the places with strange names, and sketched the Engel Inn in Himmelreich (Angel Inn In the Kingdom of Heaven) and went to the Hellenthal (Hell's Valley) and I tried to sketch the Hirschsprung, which is where the deer in the story is supposed to have jumped across the gorge when the hunters got too near. The Black Forest was red and yellow and orange and scarlet when we saw it, and in Freiburg people were talking about the grape harvest. We were told about Glockenthal wine which comes from that part of Germany, one small glass of which is enough to make you drunk! I don't know if this was just a tale for strangers as we did not drink any.

It was either between Basle and Freiburg or between Freiburg and Frankfurt that we travelled in a Bummel Zug for the first and last time. Bummel means 'to loiter' only it is a more expressive and more amusing word, and a loitering train is something to avoid. The trains in the Isle of Wight used to loiter, but worst of all was a Sunday train from Cherbourg to Avranches in Normandy which not only loitered and stopped, but the driver and guard sat on the bank and smoked! A Bummel Zug is a much cheaper way of travelling which is why we tried it.

Back to Christmas at Kassel

We got back to Kassel and to school and settled down for another nine months. We spent two Christmases in Germany and I cannot say that we enjoyed them. No doubt for German people who have relations it is a happy time, but we missed our English Christmas with 'stockings' in the early morning, Christmas cards at breakfast, the postman's arrival, church, midday dinner of turkey and plum pudding with three penny bits in it and mince pies, followed by the distribution of presents in the drawing room which had been locked all day. On Boxing Day we went to Mr and Mrs Olding and had another feast, and a children's party and during the holidays there were other parties. I went to eleven parties one holiday, but another time spent all the time having bronchitis. We only had short holidays in Germany. On the evening of Christmas Eve everyone in our boarding house, including the two maids, assembled in a sittingroom in which was the Christmas tree. Around the room were little tables on which were presents for everyone. The servants liked to have useful presents such as towels or pillowcases or anything else suitable for furnishing their future homes. The three Harkort girls whom Fräulein Zeidler looked after used to be given boots and school exercise books for Christmas presents! The tree and opening one's presents was very exciting and great fun - but next day was rather flat. We went to church and that was all. The German people all went to family dinner parties on Christmas Day and perhaps Boxing Day too. There were no dinner parties for us, and none of the children's parties we had in England. I loved dancing and both Esmé and I danced well so we always had a very good time. New Year's Eve was fun in the evening when everyone at Frau Von Buttlar's met in her rooms and played games and told fortunes, and at midnight drank healths with much 'Prosit Neu Jahr'. The windows were thrown open and we called greetings on to the quiet avenue looking so pretty under the first snow of winter. We went back to school directly after New Year. It was quite dark when we left home in the mornings walking over the hard dry snow. When we turned the corner by the boy's Gymnasium (Grammar School) you had to look out for snowballs. They were probably meant for their schoolmates, but the girls often got them instead. Kate would make one or two snowballs and shy them back if she were attacked, but I always loathed touching snow. This was dry snow and packed into a hard ball.

Leaving Germany for Paris - and bicycles

Tem decided that we should leave Germany in July that year 1895, when the summer holidays began. We left Kassel in July and travelled to France

Bicycling was the fashion, especially on Sundays. There were many bicycles made for two, sometimes for two men but generally for a man and a woman who would be dressed exactly alike in tweeds, baggy knickerbockers and thick stockings. We had seen a similarly dressed couple in Switzerland and thought it very strange. Of course we were used to bicycles, and bicycles with pneumatic tyres must have been in use when I was about ten. Children had tricycles with solid tyres, and although we never had one, I enjoyed riding other children's tricycles. Older people had tricycles too, but I think bicycling only became fashionable in 1895.

We used to listen to all the French conversation at Madame de la Boissière's and heard about Dreyfus and the Klondike gold discovery. It was very good for our French. Tem was always afraid that through living in Germany we should get a German French accent, which is certainly very ugly.

Christmas in Paris was not at all exciting; it was our third Christmas abroad. We told our French friends about Snap Dragon, and Madame de la Boissière said we should have it. We prepared the room, table, dish and raisins and the French ladies sat around the room in darkness to watch the English game. Kind Madame gave the brandy - and poured out a bottle of her best brandy with the result that the flames nearly touched the ceiling. There was the hottest Snap Dragon you can imagine. Of course we pretended it was the usual thing, and burnt our fingers pulling out much burnt raisins, and Tem pretended to be quite calm too, but I am sure we were as scared as the French people.

At New Year there was a Fair along the Boulevards. Along both sides of the streets were booths, and the pavements were crowded with laughing people. They were laughing at the little working models which were on a great number of the stalls of a woman sitting on a chamber. We had taken Louis Chartier with us and to Tem's horror he bought one of these, and showed it to the people in the bus on the way home. Tem was one large blush. But in Germany the comic papers were never looked at by ladies young or old, and you had to be very careful when buying Christmas cards to examine them inside as so many of them were extremely vulgar. Louis' grandmother scolded him for buying such a thing when he was with ladies, and she apologized to Tem, but in the middle of the apology began to laugh, so poor Tem was once more upset. We had seen fairs before as Kassel had a fair in the spring and the peasants came into town. Gingerbread cakes were sold and china Easter eggs held by china hares, sometimes only a hare. Why hares for Easter?

The winter in Paris was cold and damp although there were many sunny days too. I have not yet mentioned one member of our party who travelled everywhere with us - Kate's canary who was called Twee. He had a small travelling cage for journeys and when we arrived anywhere, and he was put into his big cage, the first thing he did was to have a bath and get rid of train dirt. So did we - but there were no bathrooms at Frau von Buttlar's, or anywhere that we had been. We had baths every day in our bedrooms, and when moving about used a folding rubber bath. One could always get cold water, and we heated water to take the chill off in an Etna, a methylated spirit lamp, if we could not get cans of hot water.

Maud becomes an aunt

At the end of 1895 Father's command at Port Royal came to an end and he and Marian and Rose went back to England. Hugh and Esther went to England before them, and in July 1895 Esther's first child was born, Thomas Hugh Evans. We were very proud about being Aunts. Father and Marian and Rose and a nurse all came to Paris in January and we went to their hotel to see them. It was over three years since we had seen Father and we felt strange and shy. Rose was fifteen months old, a little fair thing. Marian said she was upset with teething and the journey, but Tem took her and she looked quite happy sitting on that comfortable lap. One reason that it was so comfy was that she always wore garters, nothing would persuade her to wear suspenders, and so there were no clasps or buttons to spoil the lap. Esmé joined Father and Marian and they all went off to the south of France. Before going away, Father took Kate and me for the day to Versailles; it was a sunny winter day. We went there by train and had lunch there. We had been longing to see Versailles, especially as we had been reading French history.

It was now time for us to leave Paris (January 13th, 1896) and go back to England. We crossed by night from Le Havre to Southampton where we arrived at 6 a.m. on a winter's morning. We had three birds with us, as Tem gave me a pair of love birds when we arrived in Paris. They were dear little things and quite tame. They loved to walk up and down a little ladder in their cage, and pecked it to bits - and then I would go to the birdseed shop and buy another little ladder. We were proud of our birds but had to part with them as we were going to a boarding- school, so Tem took them to Gestingthorpe where Mrs Oates offered them a temporary home. The love birds died soon afterwards. I expect the East coast winds of Essex were too cold for them.

Back to England – School in Weybridge

From Southampton we went to stay with Mr and Mrs Olding. It was so funny to be in England again and we must have looked very foreign. We saw Harold again at last, and he was full of excitement about the Jameson raid, (an unsuccessful coup attempt against the Transvaal government conceived by the mining magnate Cecil John Rhodes.) and our 'Meck' relations were very kind. Gertrude had been deputed to get the clothes we needed for school. Tem left us with Mrs Olding and so ended her many years of mothering us (January 15th, 1896). She certainly was one of my 'showers of blessings'.

Kate and I went to a school at Weybridge, Surrey, kept by Dr Elizabeth A.S. Dawes D.Litt. M.A. Her father, Dr Dawes D.D. had had a boys' school at Surbiton, and her Mother was a German lady from Bonn. She and her elder sister Mary did their lessons with the boys so they had an early classical education. They were both brilliantly clever and not at all strong. Miss Mary Dawes was the first woman M.A. in England. When Dr Dawes was seventeen she got a scholarship for Girton but was too young to take it. She went to Girton the next year, took her M.A. degree (London) and after that took her Doctor of Literature degree (London) being the first woman D.Litt. For this she had to study medieval French. She and Miss Mary Dawes started a girls' school at Weybridge, but Miss Mary had left before we went. Dr Dawes was only thirty one when we came. The school was in a house called Lindores, but was growing so rapidly that the next term we moved to Heathlands, a much bigger house with a large garden. We had never been at boarding school and hated the idea and the loss of our freedom. I never liked the petty fusses and rules of boarding school and Dr Dawes was unnecessarily strict but got much easier as time went on. She was a marvellous teacher, full of enthusiasms, and we were very proud of her and liked to see her in her doctor's gown on Mark Days (once a fortnight) and at prize giving. There were two other resident teachers, Miss Beattie and Mlle Nautet, and Dr Dawes' youngest sister, wise Katie, was there for a short time before she went to South Africa where she married and is now a grandmother.

When Kate and I arrived we were very shy and stiff. We were told to unpack and shown our bedroom which had four beds in it. We were next asked for our sheets and silver. What sheets and silver? We had not been told that we must bring our own linen, spoons and forks, table napkins and table napkin rings. Gertrude did not know, nobody knew. So we had to start our first afternoon with a scolding. However, there was a cheerful girl aged twelve, Alice Runge, in our room and she told us that Isabel Hedley would arrive the next day and occupy the 4th bed. Two girls in the hall were dressed in deep mourning and were in floods of tears. Oh dear, we thought. Next day we were put in the charge of the head girl who was a day girl, Bessie Cobbett (Mrs Broad now) and she was very kind to us, but wrinkled her forehead a good deal when Kate criticized some of the many rules and wanted to know the reasons. The food was very plain, but what we had was good. We needed more variety, and we elder girls needed more to eat. We were often very hungry. It was quite an expensive school, in fact too expensive for Father's pay as a Captain, so Mrs Olding had arranged with Dr Dawes that I should help with the lowest form and save Father about £70 a year. Dr Dawes and Mrs Olding were friends, and Mrs Olding wanted us to be near her. She only lived seven miles away by road. Nobody enquired whether I had any aptitude for teaching! Miss Katie looked after the six little girls who only had very simple lessons, and there were never more than about eight.

They did their lessons in the mornings in Dr Dawes' study. The drawback for me was that I got less time for preparation and had to find ways of concentrating so that I could get it done. For instance, I found that one could read ten pages of history in twenty minutes instead of an hour if you <u>buried</u> yourself in the book. Even as a small child I never heard any of the family noise if I were reading.

We had wasted so much time in the German school just trundling along and now it was the opposite. Dr Dawes asked me once how I managed, and I could see she was interested. Afterwards I learnt that she was considering Miss Mason's plans of education. When I was teaching Marjorie Philipps we used to hurry up over the lessons, work hard and get them done, and be free to go out of doors. Her parents thought she could not be learning much but that it did not matter at her age and they never complained to me. When Marjorie went to St James, Malvern, and romped ahead of girls of her own age, <u>then</u> her kind and just parents told me what they had thought.

Once more I was able to have music lessons, and was very fortunate to be taught by Herr Muller, a pupil of Joachim, of the Guildhall School of Music. He came to Weybridge on Saturday mornings to teach Louise Rommel who, although only fourteen, was already a good violin player. She had a Guarneri violin, and it was a delight to listen to her practising. She and her sisters had been born in England but came of a musical German family. Their home was at Denmark Hill, and Annie Reincke and Alice Runge, who were also at school, lived there too. They were all very nice girls and had charming parents. Mr Rommel was the only one who looked foreign and had a German accent. Herr Muller was youngish, and keen, and helped me a great deal. He wanted four hours' practising, but that was Impossible. I could only manage two hours a day.

When Isabel Hedley arrived I was attracted to her at once and have loved her dearly ever since. She was a born leader and a general favourite, always cheerful and sensible. She was amusing too and used to cheer us up when I got gloomy about things. Nobody could have a better friend. She was the younger daughter of Mr and Mrs Hedley of Middlesborough, had six brothers and had been at school in Brittany for four years.

It was difficult to settle down to English lessons again and I had a few scoldings for writing English sentences in German construction. Not to be wondered at for I thought in German when speaking English. We had to speak French at all times during the week, except during lessons and at 'recreation' at eleven, and in the evenings when all preparation and the daily reading of a 'sensible' book was done. We could speak English on Saturday afternoons and on Sundays. The French speaking rule was easy for Isabel and Kate and me. The other girls spoke it fairly easily although one heard some strange French during walks when we marched along in our crocodile. It was a strictly kept rule and new girls found that they had to speak it or keep silent. Dr Dawes was a good linguist herself and probably did not realize just how difficult this rule was - but it certainly made everyone speak some kind of French and forget to be shy about it. Another rule was that we were not allowed to speak in our bedrooms - a dreadful rule for the chattering four in our room and we had to manage with signs and giggles. We had marks for our lessons, and every day was accredited with three good marks for Punctuality, Neatness and Conduct. Boarders had to be punctual willy-nilly, neatness was easy for me, it meant keeping your bookshelf and desk tidy and your chest of drawers, and shoes in the right place, and as I was obedient, although disliking some of the rules, the good mark business was no worry. There was a very clever day girl who was eight months younger than me, and she set a high standard of work. I always struggled to beat her at French, but although she spoke with an English accent and could not roll her Rs, she never made a mistake in written work. This was Sophy Sanger another old friend of mine. She was brilliant at mathematics (a brother had been Senior Wrangler) and concentrated on work which would prepare her for Newnham. Bessie, Isabel, Sophy and I were all in the 6th form with two or three other girls who were a little older. Kate was in the 5th form. Our marks were added up and read out to us once a fortnight, and once more the getting of marks became very important. Dr Dawes sent for me on my first marks day and scolded me for not being top of the 6th. I was second only and got a good scolding for this, to which I did not listen much for I thought being second was frightfully good and felt very bucked about it.

Kate and I had not yet been confirmed - we thought about it while in Germany, but as it meant travelling to another town where the Bishop of Northern Europe was holding a Confirmation Service, we decided to wait until getting back to England, as travelling on one's Confirmation day would be so disturbing - and after all this happened to us. Dr Dawes prepared us most carefully and once a week we went to a service for Confirmation candidates in the parish church, St James. Mr Money was the Rector of Weybridge and we liked his services and everyone thought him a wonderful preacher. Poor Mr Money got into trouble later on, but I remember his helpful addresses, and how kind he was when we had to interview him in the Vestry. St James was a beautiful church and sometimes we were allowed to go there for a treat. Our church was the Chapel of Ease opposite the front gate of Lindores and the back gate of Heathlands. It was rather ugly but of course it was very nice to have a church so near. We had a very good church education, for both Dr Dawes and Miss Beattie were devout churchwomen, so much so in Dr Dawes' case that she made us go so often that we wanted to stay at home. The whole school used to be marched to church on Saints' days at 11 o'clock. The boarders always went at eleven on Sundays and again for Evensong. You were supposed to choose whether you went in the evening or not, so one Sunday I chose not to go, and was sent for to Dr Dawes' study to explain my reasons. I had no reason for not going, but realised that the choice had better <u>be</u> for church going. We had Bible reading and prayers in the evening. We sat round the dining room table and each boarder had to read three verses of the Bible. We only thought about getting through our verses without stumbling. We nearly collapsed into laughter when one poor girl had to read 'I will spew thee out of my mouth'. Spew was a new word to her, and she said 'sp - sp' over and over again blushing furiously. 'Cut off thy hair oh Jerusalem' was another upsetting sentence.

Dr Dawes taught Scripture to the 6th form and also Church history, and I wish my children could have learnt from her too. She was a scholar. Latin she knew thoroughly and Greek was her favourite language. She spoke Modern Greek too. Our Bible lessons were most interesting. She explained different translations and we were thoroughly well taught, and Church history was one of my favourite lessons. We learnt this from a text book, but she made it all live. Every girl in the school learnt about the Persecutions, Church Councils, Crusades, Saints, Martyrs, Heresies etc., not only about the schisms and reformations of the 15th and 16th Century. I wish the P.N.E.U. would make this one of the more important subjects; it seems to me a necessary subject for all Christian children to be taught. On Sundays breakfast was later and we did not have to practise. After we had made our beds we all had to go to the 5th Form room and learn Scripture, then we went to church and after church learnt a hymn. This hymn learning stumped me and I was brave enough to go to Dr Dawes and tell her so. I can learn by heart, but some of the hymns chosen for us to learn seemed impossible. You know the kind of hymn that I mean. After midday dinner, when we always had roast beef, we were free. We went for a walk or in summer time sat in the garden and read 'Sunday books' or in wet weather sat indoors and read. At four we went to the drawing room and had tea with Dr Dawes and ate slices of bread and jam. Then we sang hymns with her, and that was rather fun for we could choose the hymns. Miss Beattie's favourite was 'Blest are the pure in heart' (which describes dear Miss Beattie) and Kate's was 'Holy, Holy, Holy, Lord God Almighty' and Mabel Ivens' was 'Oh Jesus I have Promised'. (By the way, until I was quite big I always thought the 'Eternal Father Strong to Save' hymn was about my three brothers and used to sing the brethren save verse hard for them). Then we went to Evensong. When we got back from church we each ate one rock cake and drank some water, and went to bed. The younger girls did not go to Evensong and were in bed already.

On Sunday we put on clean underclothes and wore Sunday dresses and our best hat and coats. We had no school uniform, but just as we went to Weybridge (I think it was then) we started to wear school hats and a school ribbon. The hats were black felt in winter and white straw in summer, the plain 'boater' straw that was the fashion then. The ribbon was the same colour as Dr Dawes D.Litt. gown, russet brown and scarlet.

Most of the girls wore large white pinafores, even Isabel wore them, but Kate and I had left off pinafores when we went to Germany so we had none. Dr Dawes was very particular about our hair and used to want every girl to have perfectly kept and shining hair - with the result that we had to brush our hair so much that most of us looked like hair restorative advertisements. Isabel's hair was fine and lanky and although everyone would help her and give her a quick brush as she was rushing from the cloakroom, it used to get into rats' tails so quickly and then Dr Dawes would be cross. We had to tie our hair ribbons neatly and never have crumpled ribbons. At 5 p.m. we all changed our dresses and put on evening hair ribbons. On Thursdays we put on our best evening dresses and shoes and went to the drawing room and sewed, and had supper, which consisted of a boiled egg and bread and butter. We spoke English and Dr Dawes would be cheerful and chaff us, but everyone was on their best behaviour all the same. Once a month a hairdresser came from Surbiton to wash and trim our hair and see that it was growing properly. We knew him as we had been to him when staying with Mrs Olding whom he presumed to be our Aunt, for he always said 'How's Auntie?' When I appeared for my shampoo I had quantities of hair which was cut to my waist line. It was straight, and I plaited it in two pigtails at night or in four pigtails when it had to look especially wavy. It was very heavy. When I was little it was the fashion for girls to have short hair, cut like a boy's and generally parted in the middle - no talk about shingles and bobs and crops - just ordinary short hair. I had long ringlets and our Nurse (not Blanche) used to drag the comb through them and hurt me, I can remember getting up at the Rectory before she was awake, and trying to brush and comb my hair so that she would see it had been 'done'. Esmé and Kate had had their hair cut and I wanted mine off too and was told to ask Father's permission. He agreed and one of the Aunts (Aunt Nora) took me to a hairdresser and the long curls were cut off. I can see them now, lying on the floor, and thinking what a silly I was. My hair stood straight up on end and a round comb was bought which was worn like a snood and kept some of the unruly hair flat. My hair was never cut off again and it never curled again, but still looks like Struwelpeter if I do not wear a hair net.

I have wandered again from Weybridge. The elder girls were called at 6.30 a.m. by the housemaid who lit a small open jet of gas. One jumped up and rushed to get a bath. It was supposed to be a cold bath, but as cold baths always gave me chills I used to run a small amount of hot water and say nothing about it to authority. There were rules about having a bath which I keep to this day. Dry yourself in the bath, step out on to your bath towel so as not to make the bath mat too wet for the next comer, and wipe the side of the bath. There was a washstand with a big screen around it in our bedroom, so one could dress and wash one's teeth in privacy. There was just time to brush one's hair, say prayers, and turn back one's bed, and by 7 a.m. you had to be ready to begin practising with fiddle in hand. Either Miss Beattie or Mademoiselle was there at 7 to see that all the early birds were in time. Piano players were luckier than violin players as pianos have to be in more or less warm rooms, but the fiddlers were not so fortunate. I can remember having to practise in the cloakroom and for a long time I did early morning practising in the big assembly room, almost dark in the winter, and one smoky fire just lit which never made the thermometer rise. Prayers were at 7.45am followed by breakfast and if there was porridge you could eat salt or golden syrup with it. There were large loaves of 'home made' bread, butter, cold or hot bacon and a huge pot of weak tea. Directly after breakfast we made our beds, two girls making their two beds and the two eldest girls (Isabel and me) making the little ones', or else Alice Runge, who always slept in the same room, made them. They had to be done quickly and neatly, if not, Mademoiselle would strip the beds and you had to do them again. Then rush to the cloakroom to get ready for a walk. We walked in a crocodile and could choose with whom to walk, but all conversation had to be in French. We nearly always went the same way. On getting back, change again, tidy hair, and go to school prayers at 9.20 am. Lessons began at 9.30 and there was a 'break' for drilling and recreation about eleven. We changed into black tennis shoes, and went to the playground for drilling, which was done with wooden dumbbells. Then we had a short period of recreation when we used to play twos and threes etc. and Isabel taught us Hop Scotch and Tip Cat. Then back indoors, change shoes and more lessons until 12.30, when we went for yet another crocodile walk. Sometimes we walked to 'America' which was a path to Oatlands through many pine trees. Very fine pine trees grew everywhere at Weybridge and they looked beautiful in evening light when the sun shone on their trunks. Our 6th Form room looked out on the lawn and garden and some of these big trees, and I often looked at them for inspiration while doing my lessons. It was not a crime to look out of the window as it had been at the College!

After the second walk once more we changed and washed and brushed hair, and had dinner at 1.30 pm. and we were quite ready for it. The food was good, but we always knew what we should have each day. Thursday was roast pork, Friday was fish, Saturday was an indigestible hot pot called 'Resurrection Pie' by us - and so on every day the same food. We did not have enough fruit, or salads - or variety. No cheese - no coffee. We were allowed no sweets and no cake except the rock cakes for Sunday supper. We were not allowed to have any 'tuck' sent to us. Dr Dawes ate very little herself and I do not think she realized that the want of variety was so boring, nor that the older girls needed something substantial for supper.

I had to hurry over dinner and leave before anyone else had finished and practise my violin until 3 o'clock. This afternoon practising was done in a wing of the house right away from all the schoolrooms, so one could practise hard and not annoy anyone. At 3 pm. I went back to the 6th Form room and did lessons until it was time to go to our bedrooms and change for the evening. We changed our dresses, shoes and hair ribbons and then had tea. There were the large loaves and some cut bread and butter, and jam. We were not allowed to put jam and butter on our bread. After tea there was recreation, when we played tennis in the summer or played in the assembly room in cold weather. At 6 pm. we all had to do preparation in the 5th Form room, read a serious book and do sewing, and at 7.45 pm. or 8 p.m. we went downstairs to the dining room for our supper. This consisted of cold water, a very little poured into the tumblers known as 'water famine' and either half an orange, which one sucked and bit at the best one could, or three dates. Sometimes if the midday sago pudding had not all been eaten, we were given this instead of the fruit. It was cold and stuck to the plates. This for me and for some of the others meant no supper, but some of the girls were so hungry that they would eat our portions - there was only a dab of pudding on each plate, so they did not have too much. Next we had Bible reading, New Testament, and prayers. The younger ones went to bed early. After prayers we went to the 5th Form room. Some of the other girls went to bed at 8.30 pm. and Isabel and I were left alone to do our needlework until we went to bed at 9 pm. Once a week we had a hot bath at night. Lights were put out at 9.30 p.m. Every boarder had to lie down for half an hour a day, and there was a time table for this too. There was a reclining board in the 5th Form, with a little cushion to put under your neck. The board was polished, it was hard but lying down was a comfort and we read as we rested. On Saturday mornings we would sometimes lie all over the floor so as to get our rest done. We did no lessons on Saturdays, but it was quite a busy day. We did our mending, practising, wrote letters, had violin lessons and went for a walk to the village when we were allowed to do our shopping. On Saturday afternoons we played tennis, and looked after our gardens (each girl had her own flowerbed) and sometimes went out to tea.

A weekend with Uncle George and Aunt Carrie

Uncle George and Aunt Carrie were now living at Elmwood, Petersfield, between Petersfield and Liss. We had only been a short time at school when they asked us to spend the weekend with them, and rather reluctantly Dr Dawes let us go. Uncle George and Aunt Carrie knew her parents when they were living in Corfu. We had never been to Elmwood, and had not seen Uncle and Aunt for many months, and were so thrilled to be off. Weybridge and Petersfield are on the same railway line so it was an easy journey, when we were packing, Mademoiselle refused to let us take a change of dress much to our chagrin. I do not know why she did this; it was hard on us and on our hosts. However, being with Unc and Aunt was bliss and we were very happy. They were annoyed that we could not change for dinner and never forgot how their poor nieces were forbidden this. We slept in the room that used to be called Aunt Mary's room and had a fire in it morning and evening. I can see Kate standing in front of the fire in her drawers saying that was the part she wanted to warm. We had to leave very early on Monday morning and, got back rather late for school, but having that short break away from school was a great treat.

A visit from Harold

Harold came to see us one afternoon - no - I think we went to see Mrs. Olding and Harold was there and brought us back to school. I can remember that Dr. Dawes and her sister thought he was a very nice young man. And so he was! He passed all his exams with 1st classes and was made a full blown Lieutenant of one year's seniority. Tom had done the same. They were both very clever and very hard working and very kind to us.

Lent at school

Most of our first term was in Lent, when we found we were to give up jam and go to extra weekday services, and say litanies of Penitence at school prayers; I found eating the school fish rather difficult. I never could eat salt, and this was very large and salty and hard to put down. A sauce was served with it which was also salty. Of course I had to eat it and never said anything. After I had been some time at school Dr Dawes found out that I never took salt and asked me to put some at the side of my plate, as it was a rule that we must take it. I have always thought that I must have lots of salt in me and not need any more. My cousin Gilbert did not eat it or Bernard Head either.

Easter came on April 5th that year. Some of the boarders went away from Thursday to Monday evening, but Kate and I stayed at school. On Good Friday we went to Mattins, and afterwards started running about in the playing ground but were seen by Mademoiselle who called us in, and scolded us well for irreligion. She read a sermon to us, which was then followed by a three hour service. After that we went for a nice walk with Dr Dawes through the larch woods of St George's Hills, a hilly and wild part not far from school where there was a view. I forget if there was any more church that day. But I remember the salt-fish we had for dinner, real salt salt-fish, No doubt all right for salt eaters but a penance for me. Next day was my 16th birthday. We had all been asked out to tea, but were not allowed to go which we thought unkind, as the other boarders had been allowed to go away. Once more I think it was Mlle Nautet who did the forbidding, not Dr Dawes. We dreaded Easter Sunday and expected more gloom, but imagine our surprise on coming to breakfast to find flowers on the table, a flowering plant by Dr Dawes' place, and Easter cards and eggs for us - and Dr Dawes all smiles and fun.

Confirmation

By now I had made many friends at school and liked most of the girls very much. Miss Beattie was a dear and I always loved her. She was really a good Christian and always cheerful except when school rows were going on, when she looked grieved, but cheered us up as soon as possible and always was loyal to Dr Dawes and assured us that Dr Dawes must know best. Kate and Dr Dawes were mutually attracted to each other; in fact Kate was very fond of her. The Easter holidays came soon, and we went to stay with Mr and Mrs Olding for a few days. The Confirmation at Weybridge took place at the beginning of the holidays, so after all we had to travel on that day. Tem stayed with Mrs Olding too, and they both took us that morning to school. We changed there into our Confirmation dresses and Bessie Cobbett helped us dress and to put on our veils. The dresses were of light cream crepe stuff, made with wide full sleeves with stiffening inside, and trimmed with yards of satin ribbon, long bows on the shoulder seams, and ribbons and long bows at waist. They were pretty dresses. Our veils were big squares of white net hemmed with silk, just like bridal veils only smaller. We all drove in a closed landau to St James' Church and were handed over at the door to the Rector. He put us into the front pew on the south side of the centre aisle. The Bishop of Winchester, Dr Randall Davidson, who was later Archbishop of Canterbury, confirmed us. It was a beautiful service and made a great impression on me. The lovely voices of the choirboys sang –'Come Holy Ghost our Souls Inspire' as I have never heard it sung since, and all the music was beautiful. It was a long service with 400 candidates to be confirmed. Invalids were confirmed first, then the boys, then the girls, and as the girls in the back pews went up first, Kate and I and one other girl in our front pew were the last. We had been kneeling for a long time and felt very faint by then. When we came out of church the bells were ringing and St. George's flag was fluttering from the tower in the bright sunshine. As we drove away I caught sight of Aunt Bessy and Dolly standing in the crowd looking at us. We did not know they were to be at the service and were glad to see them. Then back to school, change, have lunch still feeling quite dazed, and off to the station to travel to Southsea.

With Father near Portsmouth

I must explain why we were going to Southsea. Father had not been long on half pay, and was now Captain of HMS *Inflexible*, a battleship, and also Captain of the dockyard at Portsmouth. He had leased a house at Southsea, and he and Marian, our stepmother, and Esmé and Rose were living there. Kate and I were to spend the rest of the Easter holidays with them and stay with Marian for the first time. The house was not near the Front, but it was a comfortable square house, afterwards turned into a Home of Comfort for the dying. I forget the address. We were very tired and longed to be quiet but had to be on our best behaviour. After dinner we asked if we might go to bed and when Father asked why go so early, said we had been confirmed that day and he said he had forgotten all about it. It was nice seeing Esmé again. She was just eighteen and quite grown up in long dresses with her hair up and wearing eye glasses instead of spectacles. She always wore glasses because of a bad astigmatism which causes a squint. She took us to early Service the next Sunday for our first Communion. I remember wishing we had one of our Motherly Aunts with us and Kate told me she was so nervous that although she took the Chalice she was so frightened that she handed it back to the priest.

I loved making friends with my step-sister Rose, who was eighteen months old and ready for peep-boo games. We used to go out for walks with her nurse and the pram. We were two gawky schoolgirls and Marian must have found us very dull and she was quite different to anyone we had ever met. Father was almost a stranger too, but he always had great charm and was kind to us. Esmé talked about the South of France and Biarritz and some French friends having drawers with enormously wide frills trimmed with lace and of how she had tried on a pair. Esmé always enjoyed the thing of the moment and liked strangers and lots of changes. She was going about with Marian to parties and paying calls, and seemed to be all right.

Maud passes Oxford exams

It must have been about now that the results of the Oxford Junior and Senior Exams were published. I had passed the senior with distinction in German! What a relief as I really never hoped to get through. Grandmother wrote me a letter of congratulation which pleased me very much, as she was getting very blind.

Back to school

Kate and I travelled back to London by ourselves and went to Heathlands for what was to be her last term. It was decided that she must live in a bracing climate which Weybridge certainly is not. The chief excitement that I can remember that term is the celebration of Dr Dawes' birthday in November. We had a whole holiday and prepared an entertainment for her, carefully rehearsed charades arranged by Miss Beattie who had much acting talent, or at least encouraged us all to act our best. I remember there was a duel in one of these little plays between Isabel and me, dressed in Sophy Sanger's brothers' trousers and coats, and we were plump school girls we did not look a bit beautiful. We learnt recitation with Miss Beattie and scenes from Shakespeare and in most years presented a play at the end of the summer term. When Dr Dawes invited her friends to a Matinee Musicale we had to play or recite or set some Shakespeare. Acting in ordinary clothes with no scenery is not easy. I am very grateful to Dr Dawes and Miss Beattie for encouraging us to act, for not only was it fun and brought me enjoyment after I left school, but it has been such a help in conquering shyness and nervousness when speaking in public. I have not conquered the nervousness but can disguise it.

Christmas with big brothers in London

We spent Christmas in London where Father and Marian and Esmé were living. I think Father's promotion to Rear-Admiral (October 27th 1896) must have been about then. Christmas that year was quite different to the old days. Father and Marian went out, and we should have had no Christmas fun if it had not been for Tom and Harold, Tom provided a goose and a little plum pudding and crackers and the five of us had such fun together. Harold was in lodgings somewhere, I don't think Marian liked him so he could not be in the house. He was twenty one then. We had lots of jokes together and never noticed what time it was and suddenly heard a cab drawing up outside the house. We three rushed upstairs to our rooms in the dark and listened to hear what happened. We heard Father ask Tom if the girls had gone to bed and heard Tom say yes. I don't know where Harold was, but all seemed to be well and we never heard anything of our 'crime'. It was so funny undressing in the dark without making a sound.

Kate parts from Maud and goes to school in France

One treat during those holidays was going to the Pantomime and seeing Dan Leno. After New Year Kate left for her new school at the Chateau de Nordausgues, 21 miles from Calais towards St. Omer. We had seen the prospectus of the school but none of our friends knew, and poor Kate had to plunge into the unknown. She and some other English girls were to assemble at Victoria Station and be conducted there. We went to see her off, and a smartly dressed lady met us and made some goo goo eyes at Father who thought what a pretty governess. He had not realized that she was the headmistress. It was the first time Kate and I had been separated and we were pretty gloomy, but I was so sorry for her and it was horrid to see her go. We wrote constantly to each other, and she never complained about anything.

Maud Back at Weybridge School as Head Girl

I went back to Heathlands and to all my friends and interests. I was head girl now, as Bessy Cobbett had left in July, and in September I had to be head girl. I was a few months older than Isabel, who would have made a far better head as she was better in every way. She helped me and would always back me up. At the beginning of every term the new girls had to come to the 6th Form room and have the rules explained to them. Some of the new girls were very uppity and terrified of the head girl who was only doing her duty, but Isabel was always there too. It was hard to explain about 'The Badge'. This was a wide piece of white ribbon, with 'Well done' embroidered on it in gold coloured silk, which was worn like a royal order over one shoulder and tied at the opposite hip. Badge owners had to wear them at Mark Days and Prize Giving Days and the Badge was awarded at the end of the summer term. The girls voted for it a few days before Prize Giving and it was supposed to be given to the girl who in their opinion had done most for the school, had had the best influence and also who had most improved in character. Voting was secret, but of course Dr Dawes knew our hand-writing. We did not believe that she paid attention to our votes - or why did not Isabel have the Badge? We thought, and thought quite honestly and without prejudice, that Dr Dawes gave the Badge to a girl whose parents were friends and supporters of hers. We may have been wrong. Once two badges were given to our great surprise; one of them to a quiet day girl who so far as we knew never did anything to help anyone. She took no particular interest in games, was dull at lessons, just a quiet German girl who happened to be at school. Her mother was a great friend of Dr Dawes. The other badge winner was a dear, also in a lower form, such a kind plump large eyed girl whom we all loved, but not a school leader. After I left school I asked Dr Dawes about the Badge and she said, she <u>did</u> go by the votes, but that does not explain about Isabel. Isabel's Mother, Mrs Hedley, came sometimes to school. She called Dr Dawes 'Lilly' and talked away in perfect French. She was quite ready to criticize her or her school in a friendly way. Isabel's uncles had been at old Dr Dawes' school at Surbiton. At that time I thought it unjust not to give Isabel the Badge, but now I cannot see her being herself with 'Well done' worn on her chest.

This winter to spring term of 1897 went on, the latter part enlivened for me by visits to a dressmaker close by to have a bridesmaid's dress fitted. Gertrude was engaged to Arthur Hamilton Smith, one of Mrs Archibald Smith's clever sons, and I was to be one of her four bridesmaids. His sister Margaret Smith was another, and used to meet me at the dressmaker's, when I was very intrigued at seeing the layers of thick Jaeger undergarments that she wore, all of 'natural' colour.

Feeling lonely

Father and Marian were abroad (Italy I think) and I was written to and told to go to a boarding house in the Cromwell Road for the Easter holidays. While Tem lived with us we always had a <u>home</u>, but ever since then we never knew where we were to go and it made one feel lonely. The other girls all had settled homes and parents who welcomed them, but Kate and I had to do without. No doubt it was more training for our characters and it has made me know how children long for security. It must have been difficult for relations to interfere now that Father had married again. Dr Dawes was kind about the boarding house and said perhaps I should like it. In the end she or someone must have spread the news, for I did not have to go there after all. I went to stay with Tem at Gestingthorpe. She was staying in a farmhouse near the village and sketching. It was so cold, icy East winds, and she kept me a good deal indoors. We spent the Sunday with Mrs Oates and I remember how cold that big house was. After four days I went to Meck for Gertrude's wedding, then to Denmark Hill to stay with Annie Reincke and her kind parents for two or three days - then somewhere else - so the holidays were very happy. I was with the Oldings for my seventeenth birthday and Mr Olding gave me a silver glove buttonhook and read me a poem, and they also gave me a black leather hat box with my initials on it.

Gertrude's wedding

Gertrude's wedding was great fun, and being in the house and running up and down stairs and helping generally was all delightful. Gertrude had very thick black hair down to her knees, and wore it in plaits at the back of her head. She was not pretty but had such a nice face and looked her best in her wedding dress of thick cream silk. I saw her in Aunt Bessy's room when she was dressed. Dolly and I drove together in a carriage and pair to St. Bartholomew's the Less. Uncle Blomfield was

Vicar of this old church in the City. There was almost no congregation on Sundays, as only a few charwomen and caretakers lived in the parish. There were Grinling Gibbons' carvings, very lovely. Anything of his always interested me as I read 'The Carved Cartoon' ever so many times as a child and the hero of this book is Grinling Gibbons. When St. Bartholomew's Church was pronounced unsafe and the church demolished, the carvings were moved to St. Giles' Cripplegate, and I am now afraid they may have been destroyed when the Germans bombed St. Giles. I must go back to the wedding where I left Dolly and me in the carriage. We wore green and white striped crepe stuff dresses, the green a mignonette green, with folded belts of green silk and puffy white jabots. Dark green straw hats trimmed with light green and white ostrich feathers. Our bouquets were pink carnations. Dolly was very thin, and made me giggle by saying it was the first time in her life that she could not see her feet, the frilly jabot thing on our chest hid them! Margaret Smith and Emily Smith a niece (daughter of Walter Smith) were the other bridesmaids. We were a mixture, Margaret was tall and fair and stout, Dolly very dark and thin, behind them came Emily and me, Emily very thin and dark and small and looking vague as she always did, with a wisp of dark hair hanging down her back, and a fat fair schoolgirl - me. Uncle Blomfield married Arthur and Gertrude and was very nervous. Tem was there, wearing a short black cape covered with beads with a ruffle round her neck. The reception was at Meck, and I remember seeing lots of relations and thinking it all a lovely party. When Gertrude left she gave her bouquet to Miss Nelson to take to Mrs Nelson and Miss Nelson got coy and told us the porters at Waterloo would think she was a bride. As I thought Miss Nelson quite old this seemed frightfully funny to me. I left soon after for Denmark Hill still wearing my bridesmaids dress. We went to dinner that evening with Mr and Miss Rommell and Dr Dawes was there and had to hear all about the wedding. There was quite a colony of German people at Denmark Hill and they had their own church there.

Excitements: Diamond Jubilee and a Shakespeare play

The next term was the summer term and three great excitements happened to me. Queen Victoria's Diamond Jubilee Procession - the Diamond Jubilee Naval Review - and we acted 'As you Like It' in the Village Hall at Weybridge. I stayed again at Meck for the Jubilee Procession. All London was decorated and having a holiday. It was gay and very hot weather, and everyone happy. Dolly and I went on the Sunday to see Ida, Arthur's wife, who had just had Susie - I think they lived In Chelsea then, anyway some distance from Meck. We came back on the top of a bus, and it took an hour going along Piccadilly - Flags and decorations everywhere. I remember the Baroness Burdett Coutts' house was covered with flowers. There were illuminations at night too and the traffic stopped. I can also remember the 1887 Jubilee, and being taken to see the illuminations and Tem and another grown up held my hands and my feet were often both off the pavement. Both my top front teeth fell out on a crossing and they would not let me stop to pick them up! On Jubilee Day itself Tem got up at 4 a.m. so when I woke up there was no Tem to be seen and I cried. Esmé and I amused ourselves that day by 'playing with water' in the garden. It was also a hot day and I played in the shade of the house with little pots of water. This was forbidden and I knew it, and had to confess the sin to Tem afterwards. When I was grown up I asked her why water was forbidden and she said it was because I always made myself wet and that meant a chill and perhaps bronchitis.

In 1897 there were all sorts of rumours about the Queen but whatever happened people meant to have their procession. She was supposed to be ill, to be dead, to be going to have a 'double' go for the long drive, or best of all that a dummy Queen was to sit in the carriage. Nowadays when we can read her letters and diaries and the many lives of her, we know that it was a great ordeal for her, but partly caused by her refusing to allow her subjects to see her on ordinary occasions. She was an unseen unknown Queen and not popular until she did take that drive. I had seen her once at Cowes, no, not seen her, only the extraordinary hat she wore; it looked like a clergyman's squash hat tied on with a black ribbon. She was very short and could not be seen in her carriage. I was lifted up, but all I saw was that disappointing hat. (I was seven then). We had seats in the stand where the Carlton Hotel was nearly finished, nearly opposite the Senior United Services Club, with a good view both ways.

Tem was there and Ethel and Aunt Nora supplied us with lots of food, so we were quite a party. It was a warm day with a grey sky and no wind. There was so much to watch and the hours flew by. Hundreds of people hurrying to their seats until every stand and every window was full. Then police began clearing people off the road, and we could hear a band playing. At last the head of the procession appeared, led by tall Captain Ames as history says, but led by a fox terrier when it passed us - and everyone laughed and felt happier than ever. Captain Ames was the tallest officer In the Army - the tallest in England having being measured at six feet 8 inches. Sir Ivor Philipps was 6 ft. 5 in. but he was in India. He was followed by Companies of every kind of regiment from all over the Empire. As one band passed out of sight another appeared. Horsemen, carriages, flags, music - on and on. We had illustrated programmes so knew who and what we were looking at. Then in the distance to the West we heard a low noise, which grew and grew. It was the crowds cheering the Queen. Royal carriages were passing now, royalty on horseback, Guards, and that tremendous roar of cheering, a contralto bass roar - not a screaming noise - and the Queen's carriage passed. She was sitting alone, high up in her carriage drawn by the eight cream ponies, and two ladles sat with their backs to the horses, the Princess of Wales and one of the Queen's daughters (Princess Christian). The Queen held up a parasol, and wore a black and white bonnet - and so she passed in that tremendous roar of greeting.

Uncle Blomfield was a Prebendary of St Paul's Cathedral and stood on the steps of St Paul's during the short service - the Queen remained in her carriage and then drove on through South London. It was a marvellous show. Another day we were in the Park where we had been to see the carriages and all the grand people, and walking towards Marble Arch I recognised the Empress Frederic driving by and I curtseyed and got a smile and bow from her 'all to yourself' as Tem said, who had not seen her in time. What a thrill it all was. Poor Kate missed all this, and Father and Marian and Esmé were abroad too.

That July 1897 we were busy rehearsing 'As You like it'. Miss Beattie was stage manager and producer, Isabel was Rosalind and Bessie was the Orlando, although she had left school a year before. Several of the girls were very good in their parts and Miss Beattie chose the right girl to fit the part. I was Jacques. Dr Dawes took some of us to a professional theatre costumier at Covent Garden to choose the dresses which were hired for the day. The hose were shown to us, long stocking affairs which end at the waist, and then the man said 'You will need decencies'. 'Oh yes' said Dr Dawes, completely taken aback, and we found that decencies was the theatre name for the short wide puffy bloomers that were worn in Shakespeare's time. I had brown trunks and decencies and tunic, and a cloak and black velvet cap. My hair was turned up underneath and looked like a page's bob. Isabel acted very well and carried most of the play, I loved my part, it is one that you can get inside of and I revelled in it. We had the play in the Village Hall which was packed with parents and friends. The hot weather had continued and it was certainly very warm in those woolly trunks and decencies. The school acted these plays for our charity at Portsmouth, an orphanage for girls.

Birth of Esther's second son

That same month Esther's second son was born, Robert Henry Evans. He was a dark baby and a darling little boy and very handsome. He was missing, believed killed, at the Battle of Bullecourt in 1917. He had been wounded in the head and went back to France after a month and then was killed.

Prize Day came, with the usual frightfully long speech, and for the one and only time in my school life I got some prizes. You had to be a whole school year at Heathlands before being eligible for a prize so, although I had been there for five terms, this was the first chance. There were no prizes at the other schools. We collected certificates at the College which approximated to 1st, 2nd and 3rd prizes, but one always lost certificates. I got prizes for History, Scripture and Geography, no French prize in spite of all the efforts! Mlle Nautet had left for some time, and our French mistress was Mlle Hubart. Curiously enough they were both badly marked by small pox. Mlle Hubart was a good teacher and I liked all the French plays and French literature we did with her. She was an independent and never under Dr Dawes' thumb. She taught us needlework too and expected very good work. I knew she did not like me, but we never had any kind of breeze. I was dull and quiet and she preferred the lively ones. We had two other excellent teachers, Professor Evans for Arithmetic and Mathematics, a short clever dear man, with a beard. He taught us English Literature too, delightful lectures. He could make Arithmetic interesting even to me. The other was Professor Bevan who taught us Physiography as it was called - all about isotherms and weather forecasting etc. I loved his lessons - not so most of his other pupils. He marked my report one term 'Facile Princeps' which was awfully encouraging and gave me that 'cloud atlas' which we have. There was a Master for senior piano lessons, a Mistress for junior piano lessons and Madame who taught us class singing. Some of the girls learnt painting and dancing too. We were quite a little world of our own, but not a completely female one. Dr Dawes' father used to stay with her, a tall handsome old man with a white moustache. His eyesight was not very good, and once when he was at Heathlands he got me to read out loud to him, his choice of books being the Koran. I read on and on those repetitions and vaguely Old Testament-like chapters - on and on and never listened to what I was reading. It was very boring, but as he knew Uncle George and as he had to be amused, I did not mind. I never heard any silly talk about boys or men at school, never any nonsense or gossip. We were all so busy and so far as I know never thought about such things.

Looking after Kate

Father and Co. were at Pontresina in Switzerland and it was arranged that Kate and I should meet at Calais and travel to Pontresina together. Then we heard that Kate had had a bad fall and was ill and could not possibly travel, and that I was to go to her school and look after her. Oh, how I worried about her, and wept in my bed at night!

Mrs Olding saw me off at Victoria and put me in the charge of some people. She disapproved of my travelling alone to Calais and so did all the relations but it could not be helped. The crossing was fine, and I sat on deck next to a kind lady, Mrs Tweedie, who talked to me. When we arrived at Calais I was met by one of the governesses and two girls from Kate's school and there was the usual Calais noise and fuss of the customs, quite bewildering the first time you have to endure it. I hoped we were going straight to the school, but the others were spending a happy day at Calais and we did not leave for some hours. There are wonderful sands there, and we rode ponies at the edge of the sea, and watched the French families enjoying themselves. We drove to Nordausques in a sort of bus drawn by big dapple grey horses. It was a twenty one mile drive and the horses had brought them in that morning. We drove on and on and arrived long after dark. I found Kate in bed looking very white and ill and as if nobody were taking care of her. My bedroom opened off hers, and we had a *cabinet de toilette* where the washstand stood. The accident had happened some days before. The girls had been taken for a long walk and had crossed some ploughed fields to look at some ruins. They were all scrambling about the ruins when the wall on which Kate was standing fell. She hurt her right knee badly, and her right hip and sprained her right thumb. Somehow or other she managed to cross the fields and then was put in a rough farm cart which bumped her dreadfully. She was very stiff and bruised. A doctor came the next day, or later, and ordered applications of *eau-de-vie* to her hip, knee and thumb! Poor Kate, she needed some coddling and feeding up as well. When my trunk did not appear in my room, we enquired, and found that the Mademoiselle had forgotten to collect it after going through the Customs, and so it had gone to Paris. I did not get it for three days which was tiresome. Kate soon got a little better - she used to say that I washed her ears more than any other part! We talked a great deal, and she would get dressed slowly, and I helped her downstairs and into the garden where she would lie for hours on a chaise longue. Her knee was the worst part and was quite stiff for a long time.

The Chateau was a house in an untidy garden, with an orchard smothered in long grass. There was a farmyard close by, and the small village was the usual village of that part of France. The military road passed through, one of those dead straight roads, with poplar trees at the side, with the kilometers marked. It was not dead flat country, just slightly undulating, and even in August the wind was cold. We schoolgirls lived in two rooms, which I remember as dark brown in colour. I suppose they had brown wood walls. The furniture was shabby and there was nothing pretty or cheerful. One room was the schoolroom, and had a trapeze in it on which we amused ourselves. The other room was the dining room. The food was very plain. We had the grey village bread to eat, and butter and there was a coarse yellowish salt in big crystals which the girls ate with their bread and butter at breakfast and tea. For lunch we had the meat from which the soup had been made, it tastes nice, and is brown and stringy. We used to have it sometimes for lunch when we were in Paris, but there we always had the soup too. There were only two puddings while I was there, red currants on the stalk or little suet dumplings with a few dried currants in them, called 'Hun's Heads' by the girls. There were no amusements or games, and we were in the garden or else in the dark schoolroom all day. Then we had good news. Helen was coming to see us, and would stay for a couple of nights. She had a room in the village and we saw her during the day. The headmistress asked the three of us to dinner with her, and for the first time I saw her part of the house, all very comfortable and pretty. We had a delicious meal of several courses and Helen thought her very charming. So she was and pretty too. Kate was able to hobble about for a bit now, although her knee was quite stiff and her leg stuck out when she sat down. I remember that Helen and I went for a walk along the Military road and saw an old peasant woman leading her cow to eat the grass by the side of the road. 'The long paddock' is known everywhere! Army manoeuvres were going on, and one day untidy French soldiers wearing heavy greatcoats were to be seen. The fronts of the skirts of the coats were looped back. They seemed to march badly, but Helen said French soldiers could march a long way in a day.

When Helen left we went back to the old routine. We went to church in the village church, where there was a dear old curé who preached a simple sermon to his villagers. Kate told me that during term time the English chaplain from Calais came on Saturdays and held a service in that dingy schoolroom. She said it did not seem like church. Well, I was beginning to be suspicious about that school. It was no place for Kate except that it certainly was 'bracing' as to climate. Kate had got depressed, but was philosophic about it all, and made me promise that I would not tell Father and Marian about the school, nor make a row, for she would have to endure it, and a row would only make things worse for her. She always was my leader, and I gave my promise but do not know if I did right. All her life until now she had lived with intellectual people and now she had to do without that atmosphere and also have her faith in her Church attacked. The headmistress and her daughter were 'verting' but this was kept a secret from Father. I felt that although the few girls and teachers that I met were harmless, they were not for Kate. She was loyal to it all, just as she was always loyal to her friends, and after she left never talked about that school.

Staying with father in Boulogne

After I had been with her a month we were told to go to Boulogne, where Father and Marian and Rose would be staying and, as Kate was much better, off we went, and she had a week's holiday. Boulogne was a picturesque old town, with a harbour and fishing fleet, and the old town built up on a hill, surrounded by wide ramparts. Father and I went for many walks together, both about the town and in the country to Winèreux etc. One cannot bear to think what it is all like now. Rose was so pretty and amusing, but was getting on for three years old then, and was a fairylike child with yellow curls and blue eyes.

Kate goes back to school alone. Cambridge exams for Maud

Poor Kate had to go back by herself to school, still lame from her knee. I had to go back to Heathlands and work hard as there was another exam. ahead, the Senior Cambridge Local, which was then a stiffer exam. than the Senior Oxford. We took Greek History instead of English as that was the choice and Dr Dawes made Greek History seem the most interesting thing in the world. This exam was held at Kingston, and it was dark again when we got back each evening, especially late once when the German exam. was held at 7.30 p.m. or some such awful hour. It was cold and dark, and I had a boil on my left arm, but we enjoyed the outings, and meals at a confectioner's. I passed this exam, with 3rd class Honours. I ought to have had a distinction in Greek History and Dr Dawes made enquiries to find out why not, and the reply said that I answered the questions too fully. No mention was made on the exam. paper 'answer shortly'. Dr Dawes had prepared us for a far more advanced knowledge of the subject, and the cross examiner punished me in consequence. It made one understand how unfair it is to judge anyone's knowledge by what the correcting examiner thinks. If he has a headache or is peevish he can wipe you out. My marks were somewhere about 98% with a huge deduction for writing too much. I got 100% for Old Testament, being lucky and having learnt by heart all the chapters set.

This term we had a fancy dress dance for Dr Dawes' birthday. She was Athene, dressed in sheets, with violets, and a little stuffed owl on one shoulder. Sophy came as a sunflower in a beautifully made dress. Some of the boarders made their own costumes, and I was Selene, the Greek goddess of the Moon. Butter muslin was very cheap, about two pence ha'penny a yard, and I made the dress of green blue muslin over white muslin. A Greek dress is easy to make. Mademoiselle did my hair to look like a Greek statue. We always enjoyed all the dressing up and acting and I was quite at home at school now and able to be more useful. I even used to go back a day too soon, my own choice, which was partly to avoid that awful first day of the new term feeling. I settled in with Dr Dawes and dear Miss Beattie, chose a comfortable mattress for my bed, and next day helped to get things ready. I shall never forget when the music mistress, a very good-natured plump lady, anxious to be of use by volunteering to fill the ink pots, filled them with floor varnish stain instead! It hardened at once and would not come out, and she had to go to town and get new inkpots. Father had told Dr Dawes that I was leaving at the end of the term and I did not know what was ahead of me. Annie and Louise were leaving, and we all had a tearful last talk with Dr Dawes, sitting by the fire in the drawing room on the last Sunday evening. Next day came a letter to say that I was to stay on and Dr Dawes made up her mind that I should try and go to Newnham with Sophy. I knew I was much too stupid for Newnham and would never pass the Maths entrance exam, but it seemed a good goal to work for, and would help me to earn my living.

School Memories

It is difficult, when writing so many years afterwards, to remember events in their right order. Watching Nanette dance while her Mother played must have been in Sept. 1897. Nanette was very slim and graceful; I suppose she was about thirteen then. Tom coming to Heathlands and taking me for a walk. It was winter and the roads and paths were covered with sticky mud, and he said Weybridge should be called D'Abernon Wadeinthemud. We walked to Stoke D'Abernon for evening service in a little country church. The text was 'Be ye followers of God, as dear children' - and the walk home in England's long summer twilight. Noise and enthusiasm in the 6th form at one of Dr Dawes' lessons, Isabel and I both wanting to tell what we knew, Sophy quiet and smiling through our commotion. The rest of the school said that the 6th form made far too much noise. Getting permission to buy wooden hoops for our early morning walks in frosty weather - the senior girls and Mademoiselle and the little ones tearing along the 'route de Walton' or the 'route de Cobham' and the middle schoolgirls refusing to be so babyish but having to run to keep up with us. Needless to say the roads were empty of traffic, although a man used to bicycle down the Cobham road freewheeling, the first freewheel bicycle we had seen. And how we evil elder ones called the cloakroom Moab because the wash basin was there and the boot room opening off it was Edom ('Over Edom will I cast out my shoe'). Miss Beattie's money box for the East London Mission into which fines for spills were put and how one day she shook it and it seemed too light to be of much use for the Mission. 'Can't one of you spill your water?'

One day the Bishop of Stepney came. He was Dr Winnington Ingram, afterwards Bishop of London for so long, a real spiritual leader to London's poorest districts. Going to tea with Mrs Archibald Smith on Sunday afternoons, when Gertrude or one of the relations was there. She knew it was my last meal, and always ordered a baked egg for me for tea, and I felt so embarrassed eating it. Sophy's parents were the school's best friends. Mr Sanger was keen about tennis and had three grass tennis courts. He helped us start tennis at school, and often gave us balls. Mrs Sanger asked us on Saturdays, sometimes several boarders, sometimes two or three of us, and Isabel and I often went to that friendly house. Sophy had two elder sisters, Alice, who had passed innumerable piano exams, and Dora, who was so amusing and happy (Leila Suffrin's Mother) and everyone did marvellous fancy work and played billiards. I have had such happy times in that house. But there are so many bits and pieces of these memories.

Uncle John died at Havenstreet in September 1897. Tem wrote and told me, and Miss Beattie found me having a weep in 'Edom'. He was such a dear, and losing him must have been dreadful for his family. Everyone must have loved him.

All grown up and living with father and stepmother Marion

Father wrote that I was to leave school for good. I have always been very grateful to Dr Dawes; she has been a good friend all these years. Her intellect towered like Mount Everest above us, and yet she was able to teach us not only lessons but that we must be good citizens and take a serious view of life and its responsibilities. As I wrote before, she became less strict as years went on, but already before I left we had more liberty. The 6th form boarders were allowed to use the big music room as a sitting room. They were allowed to read poetry instead of only 'serious reading' and also have the 'Daily Graphic' so as to know what was happening in the world. I had to say goodbye to everyone and to my sheltered life at Heathlands and start a new life with Father and Marian. Orders were that I was to go to Waterloo and have my hair up as a new hat was to be bought. Mademoiselle came to the rescue and pinned up my hair firmly and I felt like a boy with hair up and a short skirt. Hair up meant skirts touching the ground in those days; heavy skirts with yards of material in them and lined as well. To keep the edges from rubbing into holes, braid was sewn all round the hem, the edge of this doubled braid hanging a little below the skirt material. I was always falling upstairs over the long skirt as I forgot to hold it up in front, and tore the braid. The skirts of evening dresses had stiff muslin frills edged with lace tacked in. I seemed to be constantly mending braid, and sewing in fresh braid or fresh frilling. Collars were tight and so were waists, but luckily for me straight fronted corsets came in about then. These had straight busk bones in front, instead of curved ones called 'Spoonbill'. My first pair of corsets was the old shape, and whenever I stooped or did anything active those wretched spoonbills would break at the waist line and pinch one. They had to be removed and new ones sewn in, and I promptly broke them again. My straight thick hair was another trial, and until I learnt to wave it and to put on a hair net was never tidy. I had always had comfortable clothes up to now. We wore Liberty bodices which used to be called vestinas, skirts were half way down your calves and hats were held on by elastic. Wearing 'grown up' clothes was only one of the many changes.

Father had a house called The Warren in the village of Hale between Farnham and Aldershot; it was nearer to Aldershot. It stood high in a little wood and there was one of those lovely views to the south of the Hog's Back with Hindhead further off. The drive opened off a private road and this joined the Aldershot to Farnham road. It was a pretty house with big trees and a rather neglected garden which was bordered on two sides by the wood in which grew many rhododendrons. They had only just moved in I think, and it seemed a strange place for Father to live. It was only later that we realized that Marian disliked the Navy and ships. She would say that she never thought of marrying a naval officer as all her friends were in the Army.

Staying with sister Helen and husband Clifford Coffin

I was sent to stay with Helen and Clifford that April. They were then living at Gillingham near Chatham. Helen was expecting a baby, and lay in bed all the time sewing at fine shirts for the layette. She gave me the long seams of the 'long clothes' to do, and I also hemmed yards of sashes for the nightgowns. The long petticoats were made of fine longcloth which was stiff to work. Clifford took me for some walks and played the piano in the evenings. The day I left them the newspapers announced War between the United States and Spain, and for the first time War was a horrible shadow to me. It made one feel quite sick sitting there in the train staring out of the window. Just a silly emotional schoolgirl's feelings, but those feelings about War have not changed.

Bicycling again

I was supposed to be grown up, but was not 'out' and was very youthful and inexperienced in many ways. I went on practising my fiddle but had no lessons, and I read as many useful books as were obtainable and found out that Marian did not like this. Father got me a bicycle, a Rover, and taught me to ride. The first time I went out on the road with him my bicycle ran away down the hill and my feet came off the pedals. I came to a narrow corner, a donkey cart, and a heap of flints on the road for road mending. I chose the flints, and did not let go of the handlebars and the precious bicycle hardly had a scratch. Father was a great bicyclist and rode so easily. He gave us the best bicycles and made us take great care of them - a speck of rust was a sin. They cost about £18 to £22. The roads for miles around Aldershot were rough and corduroyed by the Military traction engines, so riding was often very bumpy, and Father gave us especially well sprung saddles. We did not wear long skirts or petticoats for bicycling. Everyone wore very neat clothes. We had skirts made of tweed or serge, made with an inverted pleat at the centre back, which allowed the skirt to hang straight down on each side of the back wheel. Under the skirt we wore dark bloomers. Our neat shirt blouses, with a tie in a sailor's knot, were pulled down tight inside the skirt belt, and blouse and skirt were fastened with a safety pin at centre back. Over this we wore a Petersham belt fastened with a buckle and a plain hat. If a coat was needed that had to be plain too. Men wore knickerbockers and stockings and caps. Bicycling gave freedom, and one got to know one's district and all the roads and short cuts. Bicycling picnics and gymkhanas and paper chases were fashionable. I cannot understand why it was considered proper for girls to bicycle with a young man, and not proper to go for a drive together. I never found out. Our elder sister seemed to belong to the Mrs Grundy age, but we three were modern. We had had a different education and bringing up, and I have no doubt that our bicycles helped us to escape from all the old rules about chaperones.

There was some talk about this time of my studying music professionally and living in the Music Students' College hostel behind the Albert Hall. Sir Frederick Cook MP, who had married Marian's half-sister, had given this hostel and I was taken to see it. I was relieved when the idea was given up, for I knew I did not play well enough for teaching or for concert work, and should also need an expensive violin which would be Impossible to afford, I was also frightened at the idea of living alone as I was very shy and nervous. Marian wanted me to leave home and earn my own living and I was thankful that Father did not agree with her, or if he did agree, he said nothing to me. I had been very fond of him all my life, in fact when I was little I used to hope that one day I could live with him and take care of him, preferably in Italy or the Riviera, somewhere warm, not in foggy London.

Father and Marion and a heart to heart

It must have been difficult for Father as well as for Marian to have three young daughters expecting to live with him. He had escaped all responsibilities while we were growing up. Tem and the other relations had shouldered that burden. Marian was very kind to small children and patient with them, but she did not like debs. Father and I had a talk together soon after I went to The Warren, sitting on the bed in my room, with many pats on the back from him which was always his form of sympathy. It was obvious that I annoyed Marian, and I found her very difficult to understand as she was the first worldly person I had known. Father and I agreed that we were oil and water, and I promised to do everything I could to please her. She was very kind to us sometimes and had lots of good points, and then would rub us up the wrong way and we all (including Father) would be silent. It was the only thing to do, but it annoyed her. I cannot leave this subject out altogether as it affected our lives and our characters in various ways. It was all more or less a matter of pin pricks, like her always calling Father 'Jacky' or 'Jacky-Pig'. She and Father were fond of each other but had not many interests in common. She was seven years younger but always seemed to be older than he.

To Brittany - Maud nearly drowns

In July I went to the Prize Giving at Heathlands to get the Senior Cambridge certificate. We did not stay long at The Warren and went abroad again, this time crossing at night from Southampton to Cherbourg and going by slow train to Avranches, an old Normandy town. Then from Avranches we drove to Mont Saint Michel and spent the day there before going on to Paramé which is a seaside place with very good sands and bathing just east of St Malo in Brittany. I noticed that the drivers in Normandy and Brittany said 'Brrr' with many rolling Rs to their horses instead of 'woa' and 'Yup-ya' very excitedly with crackings and wavings of the whip, Instead of 'Gee-up' or 'Get-up'. Mont Saint Michel is thrilling although even then rather touristy. Some pieces cannot be spoilt, however, and there is so much of beauty and interest there. A long causeway had been built over the quick-sands and we drove over this road. The quick-sands are dangerous, and the only way otherwise is by boat at high tide. Mont Saint Michel stands out towering over the sands, high buildings on a great rock, and some distance from the shore. We enjoyed being at Paramé as the bathing is so good there, and as Esmé and Father and I were all good swimmers we had fun. One stormy morning Esmé and I decided to bathe as usual, nobody else was out but we never stopped to consider. There were very big breakers and we dived through them and got out beyond them - as we thought. I had my back to the sea when suddenly a wave broke on me and I went to the bottom, got up, and then another wave pounded me down, up again and the same thing happened. Esmé was nearer the shore facing the waves and saw me disappear. I came up at last, absolutely breathless, and Esmé helped me in, the only damage being that the thick rubber cap tied under my chin had disappeared. Although I came up each time, I never got my head out of the water to get a breath so it was rather nasty. We did not say what had happened!

We used to go to St Malo, which is an interesting old city, high houses inside very high walls, and a port - and it is full of memories of French history. One morning Esmé and I walked in, both of us in white cotton dresses with a touch of pale blue - a hat ribbon or something, and when we got to the town we found people standing about on the narrow pavements waiting for a procession. They very politely insisted that we should stand in front, and when the procession came it was the 'Enfants de Marie' all dressed in blue and white and we realized that the kind St Malo people thought we were 'Enfants de Marie' too. Rose was with us at Paramé and used to look so sweet paddling and enjoying herself.

Helen's child is born

We next moved to St. Enogat, which is west of Dinard, which again is west and across the harbour from St Malo. While here we heard of the birth of Helen's first child, Geoffrey Coffin, so now we had three nephews.

Swimming in France

The Dinard beach was a celebrated fashionable resort and we went to see it. The ladies wore very elaborate bathing dresses with lots of frills and long black silk stockings, even parasols too, and strolled about near the sea. A few were even in the sea, holding each other's hands, with the water ankle deep. These were the style of bathing dresses which are shown in pictures of bygone fashions of the 1890s. We invented our own fashion. When we first got so keen about swimming, in about 1891, Tem made them for us in thin fine dark coloured wool. They had no sleeves and the legs were short, above our knees. The neck opening was large, with a tape drawn through it, so we only had to step in to the dress and pull up the tape. Tem made us short skirts on belts, which we buttoned on, and wore when it was considered necessary, but never when in the water. Most bathing dresses had short sleeves which cut into your arms and made them red and sore, and they buttoned down the front and the buttons often came undone. We disliked a cotton material which was the usual wear, as it also rubs sometimes and is not so good if you stay in the water for a long time. The swimming mistress at Putney Baths used to try and limit Kate and me to two hours in the water.

The Casino

While we were at Paramé I was taken to another novelty. We used to go to the Casino and watch people gambling at Les Petits Chevaux, with such small stakes that it was not looked on as 'gambling', and we also went to see 'Les Cloches de Corneville' - such a pretty gay play as sung and acted by French people. Two more new things were that large carafes of cider were served at mealtimes instead of water, and I had my first admirer. He was over forty and I thought him a friend of Marian's. When we left for St Malo to take a ship to England he drove with Marian and me in the same little carriage, but I was completely unaware of his feelings. We crossed to Southampton, and Father let me sleep on deck as the ship was crowded, the success of this being spoilt by a large dog also on deck that spent most of the night howling. Kate left school and joined us.

Maud and Kate stay with sister Esther at Penzance

We both went for a long stay with Hugh and Esther at Penzance in the West of Cornwall. Hugh was the Coastguard Officer in charge of all the coastguard stations in the west of Cornwall. They lived in a small house (small for England) built of the local white staring granite like all their neighbours' houses. Kate and I had a very happy time there and were children again. I was eighteen and she was seventeen - and quite strong and full of energy. We made great friends with Hugh, who was very kind to us in his quiet way. There were the two little boys Tom and Bobby to play with. Tom was so clever and although only three was teaching himself to read. Nobody taught him, he seemed to know all his letters and would spell out a word and ask 'What does this stand for?' and then he'd know that word. He liked us to read to him, and to repeat poetry. I loved dear round Bobby who was as even tempered and as strong and daring even as a baby. Esther was expecting another baby but nobody mentioned this to us. Hugh took us with him on his drives of inspection. We got to know the coast well from Prussia Cove and St Michael's Mount to Land's End and Gurnard's Head and St Ives. I remember a picnic at Prussia Cove and Esther letting the little boys paddle. She tied long pieces of thick string to them and fastened the ends to herself so there was no danger of an accident. We used to go for picnics and all day excursions in a small waggonette, or if we went alone with Hugh he drove a dogcart. There was so much to see and to learn about in this corner of Cornwall.

Kate said she was Cornish, as the *Implacable* had swung in the tide when she was born, and so was on the Cornish side of the Hamoaze. She <u>would</u> say Cornish cream was better than Devonshire cream, and then Father would say 'You mean Carnish'. We were called 'the foreign young ladies' - anyone who comes from east of the Tamar at Devonport is foreign - History went back to legend. There is one about the giant's wife picking up sticks where Mount's Bay is now, and throwing a stone at her husband. The stone of course is St Michael's Mount - but the <u>sticks</u> are true. There is a submerged forest in Mount's Bay. The drowned country of Lyonesse was talked about. The main street of Penzance is called Market Jew Street and so many things seemed to be B.C. at Penzance, and surnames reminded us of the Armada days, Bolitho - Jago etc. Esther's charwoman's name was Mrs Juan Benetto - she pronounced the 'J' in the English way.

Hugh took us hare coursing, which was done on foot. You wear a short skirt and thick shoes or boots, put a Cornish pasty in one pocket and an apple in the other, and are off for the day. Hugh was always keen about sport and knew all the farmers. We had to run hard at times across the little fields and climb the stone walls at top speed and it was all great fun, especially as the hare escaped. Talking of hares - while we were at Penzance, Hugh had leave and as was his custom went away to a shooting. He sent some game home, including a hare which had to be skinned and dressed. The cook had just started to do this when the knife slipped and cut her hand badly. We did not think it was a job for Esther so I volunteered to try the skinning and managed it somehow under the cook's instructions. It really was a great effort for me and I did not eat any of it!

During that visit the battle of Omdurman took place and the Sudan was conquered by Lord Kitchener, and we went to a service of Thanksgiving. There was a kind Vicar at our church and the services always seemed to be crowded. Esther never missed churchgoing. The Vicar allowed Kate and me to help with the decorations for the Harvest Festival which gave me much pleasure.

The life at Penzance was peaceful. We went for walks and took little Tom to see his beloved trains. Penzance is the last station on the Great Western Railway so there was always something for him to watch, shunting, and trains being got ready for the long journey to London. The fish train was an express. The leading occupation seemed to be fishing, next, the growing of spring flowers and early potatoes, then tin-mining, with fishing by far the most important, but I may be quite wrong. Ever so many fishing boats left Mount's Bay from Penzance and Newlyn at sunset and fished all night, and also from the other ports, St Ives, Sennen etc. Quantities of fish were sent to London every day, but it was rather difficult to buy any locally which seemed curious.

One night Hugh had to visit his coastguard stations late at night, and asked Kate and me to go with him. There was a full moon, and we drove right round the western tip of Cornwall up and down over those rather rough narrow roads. I think the idea of going at night was to see that all the coastguard patrols were working at night as well as in the daytime. The stations were groups of white-washed cottages (in one of which was an office) and here the seamen lived with their wives and families. Their houses had to be inspected by the officers in charge of each section of the coast, and all was very trim and shipshape. The whole coast of England was patrolled, to prevent smuggling and to report wrecks and be ready to rescue the ship-wrecked. A coastguard left his station and walked along the path near the beach or at the edge of the cliffs until he met another man from the next station, when he turned and walked back again.

Well here we were driving in the moonlight and getting near Land's End. The little bay and village of Sennen was next to Land's End, and when we got there, instead of a tiny village asleep except for a coastguard's man, every house had lights in it, and everyone was working hard, for a school of pilchards had been caught and the boats were full of shining silver fish. The fishermen have a lookout kept on the cliffs, and when a school is seen, like a dark patch in the sea, the boats put out with the big seine nets, put the nets around the seaward side of the fish and drag them in. Carts were being hastily filled with pilchards and taken to the salting down shed. We watched all this, and the whole scene was most dramatic and busy. Hugh told us that a ship would call in and take the pilchards to Italy where they were sold cheaply for the Friday fast days. A pilchard is like a small fat herring, and in those days was not found much east of Plymouth. Next day they were plentiful in Penzance, two for one penny or something like that, no, eighty for a shilling as we had been offered at Sennen. Hugh said they reckoned to have caught about 3 million fish that night, can it be possible, but anyhow there were unbelievable quantities. I do not remember if we saw this in 1898 or 1899 as we stayed at Penzance both years.

There were yet more interesting things to be seen in this part of Cornwall, such as the Celtic crosses in some of the old villages, or at a cross roads where perhaps there had been a village once. Sometimes only the base of the Cross was left, and they were undoubtedly very ancient even if not belonging to the 1st or 2nd Century A.D. as was said. Newlyn was a fishing village with a sheltered harbour for the many fishing boats, and even over forty years ago there were artists there. Past Newlyn there was a little village called Paul where there was a fish Museum. Hugh suggested that we should visit this Museum but we were not at all keen to do so, it sounded so very dull. However we went, and saw the marvellous collection of tropical fish caught in Mount's Bay, fish of brilliant colours and queer shapes - they had swum in the Gulf Stream from the Caribbean Sea. Palm trees were growing in the Morrab Gardens at Penzance, an avenue of 'cabbage trees', the first we had ever seen. And on Saturday mornings the housewives and maids of Penzance washed the outside of their houses. They carried out buckets of water after having shut all the windows, and with hand pumps sprayed water all over walls as well as windows. No wonder the houses looked so clean and shining.

We were very proud of our little nephew Tom and wanted to take him to church with us as he always behaved so well. When we knelt, he knelt too and was very quiet. An old lady was in front of him wearing a black cape trimmed with a fringe of little black beads, and as she was not kneeling, Tom could touch the cape. Imagine our horror at seeing that both his little fat hands were full of beads, and some of the fringe was only a fringe of black cotton. A dreadful moment and the only thing to do was to take Tom quietly out of church and disappear before anyone else noticed what he had done while the Aunts' eyes were closed.

Back to the Warren in Hale – Esther has a third child

We went back to The Warren, travelling in the London express, which 'slipped' the carriage we were in at Reading, and then we had a cross country journey to Aldershot, the sort of short journey which takes a long time. We stayed at The Warren for some time. I made a Christening robe for the expected Penzance baby in the new fashion, rows and rows of embroidery and tucks but no front panel. In November the baby came and was a niece. She was christened Bertha Helen after Hugh's only sister and our Mother, and I was a Godmother. She has always been called Nelly, for a pet name had to be found so as not to confuse her with her Aunts

Bertha and Helen. We attended Nursing lectures that winter which have been very useful to me, and Esmé and I taught in the Sunday school again.

Travails with the Sunday school

Our parish was Hale - the Sunday school and most of the village was up a steep hill, towards Caesar's Camp, and the Church was down the hill, so we got plenty of walking on Sundays. Directly after Sunday dinner we had to hurry up the hill, and I spent the afternoon with several naughty girls. They really were so tiresome, fidgeting, eating nuts, whispering to each other all the time. The only time they sat quiet and seemed to listen to my carefully prepared lesson, and I thought that at last they were going to behave - one of them said 'There's a spider building a web in your hat Teacher'. They had been watching the spider and not listening to me at all. At last I spoke to the Vicar about it and he told me that he had picked out the naughtiest girls for my class for he had been told that I was used to teaching! He praised me for keeping them sitting down, as they used to move about the room and skylark. I stuck it out until we left The Warren but disliked the weekly struggle with those fidgety children. One summer day all the teachers were taken to Winchester to see the Cathedral, Wolvesley Palace, the Round Table, etc., a delightful day. We had been to Winchester as children and been taken to Saint Cross and given the Pilgrim's Dole of bread and ale at the gate - at least I was considered to be too young to drink ale and was given water in the horn cup used by the Prince of Wales (King Edward VII). Winchester is always a joy, and that long day with Sunday school teachers was interesting. Esmé and I were dressed alike in pale grey dresses with pale yellow silk 'fronts', and I remember how pretty she looked. We often wore the same clothes, which were chosen for us by Marian as we had no dress allowances. Some of our clothes were pretty and some were neither suitable nor pretty. How I suffered from teasing when I had to wear a bright blue velvet toque trimmed with a bunch of pink flowers on the top. It was twenty years too old a style for me and I felt hideous.

Coming out

My coming out dress was very pretty, soft white figured silk trimmed with chiffon. Esmé had a similar dress, and the same dressmaker in London made us 'best' summer dresses of a soft green coloured material, trimmed with white satin covered with lace - which was the fashion. There was a wide frill at the bottom of the skirt which made it very heavy and difficult to hold up. We wore the white evening dresses at a ball at the Royal Naval College at Greenwich, where Harold was studying then. We stayed with the Paymaster and Mrs Krabbé at Blackheath that night. They were friends of Father's but we had never seen them before (Nov. 1898). When we got to Blackheath station from Aldershot on a cold foggy evening Kate had forgotten the Krabbé's address and I had never known it. Nobody knew of them at the station, and although we made many enquiries we were stuck, until a postman came along who knew where they lived. We were an hour late and had upset our kind hostess and ourselves. Harold was very kind, and did everything he could for us and got our programmes filled. I was so shy that my knees were chattering together. I could hardly speak and know I was a failure. Everything seemed black although it was all as gay as possible. I knew nobody but Harold and had never been to even a tiny dance for years. Next morning all I could remember was that dreadful shyness. Harold asked me to another Greenwich ball a few months later. I stayed with Uncle Fred and Aunt Robin at Sidcup and drove with them, and things went better although I was still very shy. Harold wanted me to look my best and asked Aunt Robin to engage a hairdresser for me, and he sent me a shoulder spray to wear. He was always the kindest of brothers. The hairdresser got to work on my masses of hair and curled and waved it with tongs, and built up a great headdress affair. Aunt Robin and I agreed that it was awful, and as soon as the hairdresser had gone, I did it again in the usual simple way, only all the waving made me feel very elegant. That shyness was a great nuisance and I know I disappointed Father and Marian who wanted us to be social successes.

Looking after baby Geoffrey

That winter of 1898/99 Clifford went to the Staff College at Camberley, and he and Helen and the baby Geoffrey, and also their beloved cat, stayed with us while they were moving. Geoffrey was a delicate little mite. I loved to nurse him and worried because he looked so ill when he was asleep. We thought that Helen and Clifford were much more interested in their cat than their son, but I expect this was camouflage of their feelings.

Doing the housework

Kate had left her school in France, and I think we were at The Warren for that Christmas. She and Esmé shared a large bedroom and I had a room next to them. They were nice rooms but very cold in the winter although they were over the kitchen wing. The weeks went by and like Dorry's diary in 'What Katy Did' it was a case of 'Forget What Katy Did'. At least I remember lots of things, all too dull to write about. It was difficult to get good maids as we were too close to Aldershot for mothers to want their daughters to come to us, for the old story of soldiers being the bad ones of the family still held good. Then Marian said we were to do the housework. Esmé and Kate were housemaids and I was parlour-maid and there was a char in the kitchen. Esmé was also cellarina as she looked after the wine and decanted it. I broke port and Sherry glasses when wiping them, as I twisted them off their thin stems. The work cannot have been done well as we had never swept or dusted before. I turned out the drawing room and took hours over it. We did this for six weeks, and when the relations heard they were very indignant, and poor Temmy cried at lunch when I told her what we had been doing - I thought it was funny. We honestly did not mind, if it were necessary, but nothing was ever explained. We were never told about income, necessary economy, household expenses, we were completely in the dark. Esmé did object that Marian went to parties and left us doing housework, and I growled that dinner had to be the same as usual, with dessert and glass finger bowls and decanters. It did us no harm and was soon over. None of us could cook or make our clothes or manage a house. We learnt to use the sewing-machine. Father loved machining, he looked on it as a game and would always machine seams or hems if they were tacked or pinned in readiness.

With Ronnie Farquharson

We made friends with Marian's nephew Ronnie Farquharson this winter. He was a mining engineer in the West Coast of Africa, and stayed with us while on leave. He was very deaf, but musical, and played the banjo and after dinner would say in his high deaf voice 'Come on girls' and we would all sing the nice silly old songs like Tavern in the Town and Brown Jug and Clementine, grouped round the piano while he twanged away at his banjo. He also taught us bridge that winter of 1898. It was a new game, up till then people played whist. Ronnie called it Breech or Bridge. He said that dummy was the gap or breech in the game. I learnt it, but am not interested in cards, and the family post mortems that followed every game decided me to keep clear of it.

Helen's Bicycle accident

In May 1899 Helen had a serious bicycle accident on the road close to the Warren. Her bicycle skidded on a stone (the roads were very rough between us and Aldershot) on the hill and she fell on her right arm and leg. Clifford took her to the nearest doctor who thought her elbow had been dislocated. She was put into a cab and the bicycle was placed on the roof and she was driven by herself to Camberley, some eight miles away. Clifford rode to Aldershot, where he was dining in the mess. He passed Father and Esmé but did not tell them about Helen, and yet he was riding in front of the cab.

A day or two later an S.O.S. came for one of us to go to Helen, because Geoffrey's nurse was going for her holiday and Helen had had an accident and could not look after him. I was sent and found poor Helen dreadfully bruised, with her arm in a sling and looking very ill. I have never seen such terrible bruises. The poor dear was up, and trailing about the house. Geoffrey slept in her room and I had him all day from the time he woke at six. He was about ten months old. Helen told me what to do for him and he kept quite well. He had to be out for four hours a day in his pram, morning and afternoon, and oh, how bored I was with those walks, for

Geoffrey slept a good deal while we were out and I had nobody to talk to. All the other nurses were accompanied by their soldier friends. Geoffrey was a pretty baby and I liked learning how to care for him. I gave him too hot a bath one morning and he cried and Helen came in and told me how to test a baby's bath water with your elbow. Clifford's Mother, Lady Coffin, lived in Camberley then, and used to come every day. She was very tall and large and rather overpowering, but always very kind to us. When she was living near the Crystal Palace she had Esmé and me to spend the night and see the famous Thursday evening fireworks. We had been twice to the Crystal Palace when we were children, but had never seen the fireworks. Some years later she wrote and asked me to tea or lunch or something, and as I did not reply, decided that I was very rude. Then her letter was returned to her through the Dead Letter Office, and she wrote to apologise for her thoughts. She sent me ten shillings 'to buy fal-de-lals', this time to the right address. This was most welcome and in thanking her I said I was going to buy viyella flannel to make a blouse. She promptly sent me another ten shillings as I was not buying 'fal-de-lals'. She died very suddenly not long after that, just as she was starting for South Africa to stay with Helen and Clifford in the Transvaal.

The Annual Ball

While I was at Camberley the annual ball at Sandhurst was held and Clifford took me to it and I had a happy evening. It was a big ball and all the different Military uniforms made it a very gay affair. One never wore pink to a Military dance, because pink clashed colours with the scarlet tunics. I wore a bright sky blue silk dress veiled with sky blue net - too bright a blue for me and I must have looked like a Union Jack. I danced with cadets who bumped one but were friendly, and also with a kind Captain in the Cameron Highlanders. He did not make me shy and his uniform was gorgeous. In fact I think he first broke the ice of my dread of going to parties and dances. Amongst the uniforms was a khaki one, carefully shown and explained to me by Clifford – 'Indian regiment - the colour of dust - invisible at a distance'. Not many months later England was fighting a khaki war.

More acting and Aldershot Balls. Bessie as chaperone

That summer I stayed a day or two with Sophy Sanger at Newnham and saw Cambridge for the first time, and she and I went to Weybridge for a few days. Dr Dawes asked me to help her with the school play 'The Lady of Lyons' and take the part of Claude Melnotte the hero. It is a romantic old play about a peasant boy who becomes one of Napoleon's generals and is in love with a young lady of high degree, all quite absurd but of course I was delighted to have the chance of acting once more, and set to work to learn Claude's very long speeches. Esmé and I were also to go to two Aldershot balls and Marion invited my middle-aged admirer of the St.

Enogat days to come and stay with us for these balls, and either Marian or Esmé must have hinted that he was coming to see me. I did not know what to do to escape. I asked if Bessie Cobbett could stay with us too, and when she came I confided in her and she promised never to leave me alone with our other visitor, Bessie and I walked about our little wood where all the rhododendrons were in flower and the primroses dying in the hot sunshine, up and down those grassy paths – no, not schoolgirl chatter, but Bessie hearing me recite Claude Melnotte's speeches. We went to the halls and came home at dawn tired out and feeling awful. Once again the uniforms were thrilling, and so were the Highland eightsome reels. I was too English to enjoy the bagpipes or the yells of the dancers, but it was interesting to see if not to hear, and you did not have to make conversation while sitting out with your partner between the dances. Remember that all my partners were strangers to me except the man staying with us. Next morning Bessie had to go home, and he asked me if it were any use his staying on longer. I said No, and he left and I never heard of him again. I am glad the family did not tease me, nor scold me about him. I was nineteen and very young for my age, and he was forty-two and stout. I still did not want to be 'out' and Esmé was there to pay calls and go to parties with Marian.

I went off to school for the play and enjoyed it very much, strutting about in a French peasant's dress, a general's uniform and a pale grey satin embroidered coat and breeches for my stage wedding. Ethel Fraser, (now Mrs Merison) was my lady love, and when we were older how we laughed at ourselves for acting in such a play. I think I stayed with Mrs Olding for this. I used to go to her every year and was always so happy to be with her.

A Bazaar at Claremont

Lady Helen Vincent

She took me to a bazaar at Claremont, the small palace near Esher where royalty lives. The widowed Duchess of Albany, daughter-in-law of Queen Victoria lived there with her son and daughter. The daughter is the Princess Alice, Countess of Athlone - and is younger than I am for at this bazaar her hair was hanging down her back. There are lovely trees and lawns and gardens at Claremont, and we went into the house where the sale was, and there I saw a perfectly lovely woman. She was the Lady Helen Vincent, quite beautiful - face, figure and manners – standing behind a table selling things. We bought something from her so that we could look at her for a moment. I don't think she was young, but she was lovely with the beauty that lasts. Queen Alexandra was always beautiful and although I never saw her when she was young one could understand that older people were speaking the truth when they said her beauty took your breath away. We also saw the Duchess of Albany that day, a kind faced bulky lady. She and Queen Emma of Holland were sisters, so she was Queen Wilhelmina's Aunt.

With Sir Frederick and Lady Cook

I also stayed with Sir Frederick and Lady Cook at Hyde Park Gardens that summer for about four days. Lady Cook was Marian's half-sister, and her husband was a millionaire, a Baronet, and M.P. for Kennington which is part of London south of the river. His father, Sir Francis Cook, had made the fortune. Father always said 'he sold paper collars in St. Paul's Churchyard' and quite what he meant I don't know. Sir Francis was a collector of pictures and other works of art. I arrived in this big London house and, as Lady Cook was out, was put to wait in the drawing room which was furnished with gold chairs and gave a general impression of being gilt all over. Tea was brought in, and the butler lit the spirit lamp under the silver urn. Then the kettle boiled and boiled, and I wondered what to do and did nothing. Lady Cook came in and took charge of me and the kettle. She was very kind to me, and I trotted about after her. She was economical, one of those people who can't afford things. When we went to bed, we first went to the dining room and locked up the biscuits. At breakfast time she and I were punctual, and doled out the pats of butter, one large pat for each person, and then the butter dish was put on the sideboard so, if you wanted more, you had to get up and fetch it. Her husband belonged to the Coaching Club and when there was a Meet of the Club in the Park, her carriage horses had to be rested for a day or two before, so that they would be very fresh and excited when shown off in the four-in-hand. Lady Cook used to go about in the buses at these times, and not allow herself a hired carriage. I enjoyed driving with her, it seemed so grand to be wearing my garden party frock and driving in a carriage and pair to Buckingham Palace to 'call' after some party although we only went to a side entrance.

I went to Henley Regatta while staying there, joining a party with Marian's sister, Mrs Sisson, kind 'Aunt Lolly' and her pretty daughter Dolly Sisson, and several other people. We went by train, and when we got to Henley I saw Dolly powdering her nose in the Waiting Room at the Station, and thought her so sophisticated. I soon learnt to do the same, we used Papier Poudrè, in little booklets of sheets of very fine paper covered with face powder. It was invaluable to use when one got very hot when bicycling or dancing.

Henley Royal Regatta 1900

Henley was so gay and pretty with crowds of boats, gay coloured dresses, green trees and rows of houseboats decorated with flowers. Aunt Lolly knew the people who owned Phyllis Court and took us there to tea. Phyllis Court was later a Club House, but was a private house then with lawns sloping to the river. Another day Marian took me to lunch with her niece, Violet Farquharson, who was Mrs Streeter Lambert, and they lived In Kensington Gore. I sat next to my host, who hardly spoke to me and made me shyer than ever, and afterwards Marian scolded me, and quite rightly, for not chatting politely to him.

At the Albert Hall

We went on that afternoon to the Albert Hall to hear Patti sing. She had retired the year before but used to sing sometimes 'for the last time'. Clara Butt sang 'Seated One Day at the Organ' with organ accompaniment, and her huge voice drowned the organ, and even made our chairs and spines vibrate. Ada Crossley sang in a lovely rich soft voice, and Ben Cavies, elderly then and loved by the audience, and Patti sang. How clear and sweet her voice was. She was slim and graceful and sang as easily as a bird 'Home Sweet Home'. I am so glad I heard her even though people said her voice had faded, and you ought to have heard her when she was young. That was a great treat that Marian gave me. She also took me to an Evening at Home at the Streeter Lamberts (Violet was a sister of Bonnie's). I was told that her dress cost £50. She sang to us and looked very pretty in the fifty pounds.

More relatives

Esmé and I stayed a day or two with Lady Cook's sister, another Mrs Farquharson, the widow of a clergyman. She had three or four young daughters and lived in a flat and was quite badly off I imagine. I can't remember much about it except that London was having a heat wave. I had seen very few people at Aldershot. It was packed with regiments, soldiers were everywhere, but generally only for a short course of instruction so regiments kept to themselves, and people went to London for their amusement. We knew a few people about Farnham, and of these was a family called Bacon. He was a Captain in the Army and we were distantly connected. Father was talking about Gretna Green marriages and said that his great uncle was married at Gretna Green. Captain Bacon said his great aunt was married there too - and they found they were talking about the same wedding. This great great uncle of mine was General Sir John Spink, the brother of my great grandmother Mrs. Fiske who was Esther Spink, the lady sitting at the left side of the Silhouette picture I have in my possession.

It was when we were at The Warren that we used to see motor cars, or at least a motor car. There was a Mr Knight at Hale who was experimenting with them. They were small and noisy and rattling, made like four wheel pony carts without the ponies, and if you saw one it was generally broken down or stuck on a hill. We left the Warren now, and except for one or two short visits I was not there again.

Father had been appointed Admiral Superintendent of Devonport Dockyard and we lived there until 1902. We three girls and Rose and her nursery governess all went to stay at a farm at Yelverton during the move. Yelverton is high, on the edge of Dartmoor, and was then a village with a scattering of 'villas' along one road. We stayed at Mrs Jones' farm where Mother used to stay with her elder children. Mrs Jones is one of the two people who thought me like Mother; the other was Admiral Cardale's wife, who was a great friend of hers. In both cases they saw me first in a dim light, so did not see my colouring. Mrs Jones came into our sitting room where I was writing and said at once that I sat, and turned round and spoke like Mother. It is curious because nobody else ever noticed it. We enjoyed Yelverton and used to go for long walks over the Moor and chase the wild ponies and Esmé, who was having a churchy period, persuaded us to go to Matins every morning. Marian's schoolboy nephew Lawrence Sisson was with us and Kate still ranked as a schoolgirl as she had not put her hair up. She and I went from Yelverton to Penzance for another visit to Hugh and Esther. This time there were three children, as Nelly was the baby of about nine months, and Bobby an adorable two year old. His cot was in my bedroom and I was his willing slave. We went for picnics and one day Hugh took us with him when he and his inspecting Captain drove to several coastguard stations. We drove in an open carriage and pair, and went for many miles. The coastguards were inspected, their houses looked at, and at one or two places they gave a demonstration of life saving with a breeches buoy which was extremely interesting to watch.

Kate and I went to Devonport when we left Penzance and settled into our new home in the Dockyard, There is a terrace of houses where Dockyard officials live. The centre house is much bigger than the others and is the Admiral's house. It has a signal room and flagstaff on the roof, a large Royal Coat of Arms on the third storey balcony across the first storey, and a verandah in front of the ground floor windows. From the front door a few steps lead to the paved terrace, and then a flight of stone steps down to the road. In wet weather the underground passage is used; a door is opened at the side of the steps and leads one underneath the Terrace and up a carpeted staircase into the hall of the house - and you can imagine what a boon this was in wet weather. The house was furnished by the Admiralty and several things reminded one of a ship. It needed new paint and papers and some new carpets, and Father and Marian had been able to choose some modern colourings instead of the usual purple red carpets and curtains. In the hall there was a beautiful model of a ship in a glass case, and also a big painting of a naval battle. The dining room table was famous. It was round and could be enlarged by adding extra curved leaves on the outside, so it could be used for 8, 12 or 16 people. If a larger table was needed, it could be made into a banjo shape. It was an old table and beautifully made and very strong.

The visitors' book was kept in the hall and we had to be careful to avoid people who were writing their names. All officers of the port and garrison (or their wives) had to write their names and addresses in the book, and that was the correct way of making the first call. If they were married we had to return the call. There were visitors' books also at the Commander in Chief's house and the house of the General Commanding the Western District. Our house had two wings at the back with a yard between, so it was much larger than it looked from the front. Father's study, the dining room and back dining room, and a little room called the Midshipmen's room, were on the ground floor and the 'offices' were what house agents call extensive housekeeper's room, butler's pantry, servant's hall and a malt house dating from home brewing days, store rooms, kitchen, scullery etc. etc, all very roomy and old fashioned with copper saucepans etc. The scullery maid whom we always pitied had to always polish them. On the first floor was the long drawing room, the shape of an E without the middle stroke. The top stroke led into a conservatory. The lower stroke was used as a morning room and could be shut off by folding doors from the drawing room. Leading off from this floor there were more rooms in the wing, bathrooms and a sitting room where we did our sewing and Rose played, and one or two spare rooms. Above again were the maids' rooms, footmen's rooms, box rooms etc. which were over the kitchen wing. On the second floor were the best bedrooms where Father, Marian, Esmé and Rose had their rooms, and the best spare room which faced the Hamoaze. The main staircase and the service staircase went up to the second floor. After that there was only one staircase. My big room was behind the Lion and Unicorn Coat of Arms, and had two windows at each side of this. They were small windows and had a splendid view of the Hamoaze and Dockyard and of the old *Implacable* and *Lion* where we used to live. Kate's room was next to mine, and there was a big spare room, and the lady's maid's room. A narrow staircase went up to the signal room where the flags were kept. The coxswain,

Brebner, went up at 3 a.m. to hoist Father's flag, and at sunset to lower it. There was a small garden at the back of the house, with a path in the centre leading to the back gate in a high wall. To reach our garden proper you went through this, crossed the back road, and through another door to an old-fashioned walled garden with vegetables and fruit and a greenhouse, and fowl run.

The Dockyard is surrounded on the landward side by a very high wall, the only entrance being through one gate, which is guarded day and night by London Metropolitan policemen. Nobody can go into the Dockyard, or out of it, without their permission. There were really two yards, Devonport and Keyham which were joined by a railway tunnel. Keyham Yard was then being enlarged, the contractors being Sir John Jackson and Co. - no relations of ours - famous contractors. In a dockyard are the building slips on which ships are built before being launched, workshops, great sheds, dry docks, basins, offices, naval barracks - and a church. There were miles of roads paved with large rough cobble stones or stone blocks, very tiring to walk on, miles of water-frontage, high piles of great squared teak trunks from Burma, a tremendous noise of machinery and electric riveting, thousands of men (dockyard maties) hundreds of foremen and clerks, a draughting office where ships were designed, a rope factory and a flag factory where women worked, anchors and chain cables lying at the side of the roads, a boiler factory which made men deaf, the reverberation of hammers on boilers being terrific, molten steel, carpenters' sheds where men worked with buzz saws and band saws and often got careless and lost one or more fingers, 'liberty men' from a ship marching up to the dockyard gates - a world of ships and ship building, ships at anchor and ships in dry dock propped up with huge baulks of timber. Steam whistles and boatswains' whistles adding to the noise, and steam launches are darting about in the harbour.

The Hamoaze, lying smooth and shining in the sun, and the peaceful rounded Cornish hills across the harbour. Anchored in the Hamoaze immediately in front of our house was HMS *Cambridge,* the Gunnery School ship. Further to the right lie two older ships moored together, HMS *Lion* and *Implacable*, now training ships for boys, the future seamen.

Our house faced west so we saw sunsets reflected in the harbour, and also felt the westerly and south westerly gales which blow often in south west England. Further up the harbour the torpedo School ship HMS *Vernon* lay in a quiet river off the Cornish side. Saltash Bridge over the river Tamar, just before it widens into the Hamoaze, was the only bridge, so all cross river and cross harbour traffic went in boats or by chain ferry for vehicles from Tor Point to Devonport. We went to Keyham yard in the dockyard train which had a compartment we were allowed to use. The Naval Barracks were at Keyham, and the School for Engineering students, and also the huge extensions being made. It is hard to describe what is all so vivid to me and yet so complicated. Vivid does describe the light that was over it all, the stretch of sky and reflections in the water. It was never dark and depressing in bad weather as a street can be. We were allowed to go about the yards and watch the maties at work, and the naval officer in charge always let us know when a ship was being moved in or out of dock for we never got tired of seeing this.

Of course we never went about alone, and always kept out of everyone's way, but as we were genuinely interested in the work we were allowed to see the wheels go round. This was the place where Kate and I had now arrived to live. I was nineteen and a half and she a year younger, and although Kate preferred to remain a flapper for a little time longer, I could no longer do so.

Tea and dinner parties

A battleship was launched just after we came, and there was an At Home and tea party for 300 people afterwards. Esmé and I had new winter dresses, soft French blue wool, with string coloured lace at neck and wrists, which suited us both. The launch was the first one I had seen, and a great thrill. It is one of the most exciting things to see a great ship poised - then move a fraction of an inch and then rush astern down the slip into the sea. After the launch we hurried back to the house for our party. Marian and the others got back first and went to see to things and Marian was tired and sat down. I had just reached the hall by the front door when a stream of people started to come in. Word was sent to me to shake hands with them as Marian was tired, so there I was shaking hands 300 times with strangers. That was my first tea party! The first dinner party came immediately afterwards. The brother of the Princess of Wales, Prince Waldemar of Denmark, had come to Plymouth in his ship, and the Commander-in-Chief, Sir Henry Fairfax, was having a dinner party for him. Father and Marian and a daughter were invited, and I was taken.

Dinner party with Prince Waldemar

They told me about Prince Waldemar while we were in the carriage, and that I should have to curtsey to him. He stood at the door of the ballroom with Sir Henry and Lady Fairfax, and we were introduced and made our curtseys. I was the only girl, and the flag lieutenant the only young man. My partner was an old white haired gentleman who enjoyed his dinner. He was not in uniform which I thought dull. He must have thought me dull, for he hardly spoke. On my right was Commander Trevelyan Napier and he did not seem to think me interesting either, but he did speak a bit. We were at the end of the long table. The Prince and the Fairfaxes and the Earl and Countess of Glasgow, who were staying with them, sat in the middle. Lady Alice Boyle was there too. She is Lady Alice Ferguson now, but we did not meet then or at a lunch party a few days later when Lady Fairfax 'borrowed' me as acting daughter. The Glasgows were in Devonport because their son, Lord Kilburn, a naval lieutenant, was very ill. He is the present Lord Glasgow, whose wife lived at Wadestown, Wellington, during the 1914-18 War, Norton and Phyllis and I stayed with her for some time in 1916. (see Book II). But I must go back to my first dinner party. After dinner we set in the ball room which was arranged as a drawing room for these occasions, and a naval orchestra played in the Musicians' gallery. When Prince Waldemar stood up, everyone stood up. When he sat down to talk to someone else, we all sat down, and so it went on, while he talked to each lady in turn - at least to the grand ladies, not to me. I talked to the flag lieutenant in the intervals of all this standing up and sitting down. Time went on and on, and the Prince made no move to go. Someone said (probably Father) that he was waiting for beer and sausages to be brought in for supper. At last the Danish flag lieutenant was spoken to and given a hint, then he whispered to royalty who stood up rather fiercely, bowed stiffly several times in various directions, while all the ladles curtseyed, and marched out. 'Now I can go to bed' said Lady Glasgow and Father skipped round the room - and off we went. It was an alarming evening for me. How awful if I had said or done the wrong thing, but although it did not cure my shyness I had found out that I could swim. The next evening there was another dinner party to which I was sent alone in charge of Father's coxswain. A daughter had been invited and Esmé did not want to go. Captain and Mrs Craigie were my hosts, and it was a private party - all strangers of course. Next to me was an elderly man (very old to me) who suddenly said to me 'I suppose you think I wear a wig, well I <u>don't</u>'. I had not looked at his hair before, and now had a look at it - a great mop of shaggy grey hair – I suppose one was meant to admire it. The man was Capt. Hammick, and when I told Father next day he laughed and said 'Old Jagger 'Ammick'! They had been naval cadets together In HMS *Calcutta* on the China Station. I don't know why he was called 'Jagger'.

Junior Officers

All the junior officers of the *Calcutta* on that commission were promoted to Admiral. The young surgeon became an Inspector General of Hospitals and Fleets, and the young Naval Instructor, who had a great influence over Father, was afterwards Sir John Knox Laughton the Naval historian. It was a great record. The *Calcutta* was the flagship of the Station, and England was then at War with China. The cadets, including Father, were only fourteen years old when they joined the ship - and the marvel is that they survived to grow up, let alone continue their careers so successfully. Father had been to school at King's College (London) before going to sea, and had won many prizes and fought many boys. He told me that the Navy Entrance Exam was simple. Admiral Morant told us that when he joined a few years earlier, all he had to know was the Church Catechism!

War in South Africa

Wandering again, I must go back to Devonport in that autumn of 1899 - and War. The South African War started and Devonport and Plymouth people thought of little else. Many of our new friends left with their regiments for Cape Town, and the 'lucky' ones in the Navy were those on the Cape Station. I cannot remember any jingo spirit; in fact many people in the Navy and Army thought it was an unnecessary war, but that it had to be fought as it had come, get it over as soon as possible and let South Africa settle down to peace. We read 'The Transvaal from Within'. Not everyone thought Cecil Rhodes a noble statesman and the Jameson Raid was wrong. Still the politicians had between them, both Boer and English, decided for war and the Army had to fight it and the Navy keep the sea communications open. One of the gunnery lieutenants on board the *Cambridge* was a Mr. Molteno, a charming man, one of a large South African family. His eldest brother had been Prime Minister at the Cape and he himself thought the war a great mistake. Harold was on board the *Cambridge* too, which was an added joy for us as we saw him constantly. He had passed all his Greenwich Exams brilliantly with first classes, once more copying Tom's achievements, and was now doing a Gunnery Course. The South African War is now history, so I will only mention it as it concerned us personally. The horrors of that War were enteric fever and starvation during the sieges of Ladysmith, Kimberley and Mafeking. We had many friends in South Africa and all who were not there were using all the influence they had to get sent out. The officers' wives and leading ladies did what they could to help the wives and families of the men, and worked for the Soldier and Sailors Families' Association.

Entertaining the troops during the Boer War

We helped with entertainments to raise money for this, and we managed to get a great deal of fun out of this form of working for the War. Mrs Craigie got up a Japanese Matinee Musical in a big hall. There were songs etc. on the platform and the hall was turned into a teashop. We girls were dressed in gay kimonos and obis with chrysanthemums in our hair, and waited. I had no luck with my table as some strange folk came to it - they spilt a jug of milk on the floor and ordered me to wipe up the mess. This was difficult to do as kimonos are long and tight, and the long sleeves get in the way, to say nothing of being afraid of spoiling my new kimono. When my customers left, the men of the party gave me a halfpenny tip! Tips were added to the fund and I had to explain the halfpenny! The Highland Light Infantry was stationed at Devonport, and Esmé had a very handsome Captain of the H. L. I. who admired her, but the regiment went away and had terrible casualties. As the weeks went on, the news of constant reverses and the long casualty lists made everyone sad - but life had to go on, and there seemed to be a rule never to mention the war or casualties at dinner. The constant dinner parties went on, as that was the recognised form of entertaining, and it would have been too trying if anyone had wanted to converse about the war during dinner. Civilians could do it, but not Navy and Army people. So many men had gone from Plymouth and Devonport and died of enteric, were wounded or killed, or shut up and besieged.

Mrs Walford, as another way of raising money for the S. and S.F.A, produced a play 'The Scrap of Paper' and asked Marian if I could take a part. Marian said I was very young for this, but should enjoy the acting, so once more I was learning a part and having a marvellous time at the rehearsals. My young man in the play was a young gunner Napper Tandy (Irish) he was great fun, very bright and clever and acted well. A Captain and Mrs Beynon were in the play. He was another gunner and she was quite young and they were very nice to me. Mrs Salford thought it would be a good thing if the company stayed with her for the week end and rehearsed hard, so off we went to her very old house on the banks of a tributary of the Tamar. It was winter and I shall never forget the damp cold of that house. We rehearsed in the hall - a real old panelled great hall, with rooms opening off it, a very high ceiling and a musicians' gallery. There was a huge fireplace in which logs were burnt, but they did not seem to give out any heat. Mr Tandy and I used to sit in the study when not wanted to rehearse, so as to get a little warmer, and the rest of the company kept on coming in to see if I was all right, and I was so youthful that I did not know why! There was another girl in the caste, much older than I, and we had two bedrooms opening off each other. The rats made a noise and she was afraid of ghosts. On Saturday evening after we had gone to bed I sat for ages over the fire in the Beynon's room talking, and then had to find my way along a curving stone passage some way to my own room and fell over various boots put out to be cleaned. Next morning at breakfast I brightly said to my hostess 'Did you hear the ghost last night?' and she replied crushingly 'We never mention it'. We were all marched off to church across damp fields and sat in the north transept of the little old village church. It was cold and damp and there was a smell - one of the parties had to take his wife out as she felt faint. We decided afterwards that we had been sitting over improperly buried ancestors. Next day we went home.

The Theatre Royal at Plymouth had been taken for the evening, and the pit turned into stalls. I got severe neuralgia from cold and draughts and had a splitting headache on the day which got worse and worse. Esmé took me to the theatre and dressed me, and I can remember being almost blind with the pain, so she went to Mrs Walford for help and she came to me with a bottle of port which I drank down. It did not make me drunk but just deadened the pain for a couple of hours and I got through my part. The theatre was packed and we made £100. There were the usual curtains at the end and flowers for actresses, and I was given a bouquet of white flowers. This was from <u>Esmé</u> as I knew, and she had done it to encourage me and also to make some fun as everyone wanted to know who had sent it. Father asked me several times but I never gave her away. There was a party and supper after the play, but I had to go home to bed with the neuralgia.

I was asked to act in 'Dandy Dick' the part of the Dean's younger daughter, and while we were rehearsing Mr Tandy left for South Africa to his great joy and Mr Hickson of the R.M.L.I. took his part. Father had always enjoyed acting and was glad that I was keen about it too. This play took place after Christmas and that sad 'black week' of the War, when every day we heard of defeats and the casualty lists were terribly long. There was a public meeting in the Plymouth Town Hall at Christmas time at which Father was asked to speak and he took me with him. As far as I can remember it was a sort of patriotic-cum-religious gathering, emphasis on what is called patriotism. We sat on the platform facing an audience of 2000 people. Father was the son, grandson, brother and brother-in-law of clergymen - and he hated long sermons. His address lasted about three minutes. He reminded us of Christmas, told us not to let bitter and revengeful thoughts about the Boers enter our hearts 'for when the War is over we have got to live with the Boers as fellow citizens' and I wonder if his hearers were as impressed as I was. We know now how right he was, but he said this during the worst period of the 'Khaki War', when Kipling's 'Absent Minded Beggar' was being recited at every concert and patriotic gathering all over England. We had no friends on the Continent, Holland very naturally could not sympathize with the Boers, the Kaiser was worse behaved than ever, and the French very antagonistic and their press venting its annoyance by publishing vulgarities about Queen Victoria.

We had settled down very quickly and were all enjoying ourselves. You would think us very useless girls. We could not cook, knew nothing about housekeeping or prices of food, had never washed or ironed our clothes - we could sew nicely and occasionally made a dress or a skirt. I even trimmed a hat once. We had never kept accounts nor bought our clothes. Esmé and I could each play the piano a bit, and I practised the violin. Esmé arranged the flowers; Kate helped Marian with the household books and accounts - those small red account books which the shops provided for their customers, the milkman's book, the butcher's book etc. I wrote invitations, was in charge of the Visitors' book to enter new arrivals on lists and arranged who took in whom at a dinner party. This went entirely by official rank and seniority, and dates of promotion had to be looked up in the Navy and Army lists, for it would be a terrible thing to make a mistake of only one day about this and would give great offence. I also answered invitations. I wrote neatly then and that was why this was my work, and many, many a time have I been glad of this training. There were two kinds of official dinner parties - for executive officers and their wives, and for engineer and Dockyard officials (such as Chief Expense Officer, Chief Constructor etc.) and their wives. The two varieties did not mix. We used to call the latter kind of party 'Works dinners'. At one of these there were dreadful pauses in the conversation. We all talked hard and did our best but some of the guests seemed to be shyer and more speechless than ever. Next day Father went to his office as usual, and was teased by one of his friends for having asked two Dockyard men to dinner who had not spoken to each other for eight years! Father was furious with me for my *faux pas*, but how were we to know about it? We had yet another kind of dinner party, and that was a 'Young' one. We were always allowed one lieutenant or subaltern at the stiff elderly affair, but at 'Young' ones everybody was young except Father and Marian. She generally went to bed early and we used to play Billy games and make a great noise with Father being particularly lively. We used to play 'If' and games like that. At the solemn parties we had to provide music after dinner until the guests left. I played my fiddle and Rose's governess accompanied me, and she used to play too. We thought that nobody listened to us, as the more we played the louder they talked. One time Miss Cregoe and I played the same tune all the evening. We were quite sure that no one would notice our wickedness. She played the cello too, so we had cello, violin and piano solos and trios, all the same tune. Another time Kate got hold of a Bigaphone trombone - made of cardboard, into which you boomed a tune. It looked like a trombone at a distance and she solemnly got up, asked Miss Cregoe to accompany her, and she 'booed' a little tune and waggled the stick part about. We were all surprised and longed to laugh but did not dare. Of course there was a row afterwards, but Kate got away with it,. She was never afraid of Marian and got on very well with her.

There were dances too; private dances and ship dances and sometimes a ball. We gave several dances in our house, although during the most anxious period of the War we were not supposed to dance officially. 'At Homes' were allowed. An evening At Home was a fashionable party when we were young and I still think it is an amusing way to entertain, for everyone wears best frocks, there is an orchestra which accompanies the roar of talk, a supper, and you meet your friends and their husbands. Lady Fairfax gave an evening At Home to welcome the officers and their wives of the Militia regiments who came when the regulars had left for South Africa. Giving a dance then was an easy matter for us to arrange, Esmé arranged some flowers on the mantel pieces, I sent out the invitations and the music was generally piano, violin and cello. We had a rule between ourselves that we would not dance until other girls' programmes were filled, anyway for all the first dances. Nearly all the men were in uniform, and as ships came in and left, and regiments changed too, there were always strangers. We would ask the girls if they preferred Army or Navy - and introduce accordingly. We would have about three or four young married couples, but otherwise everyone was unmarried and Marian was chaperone. A ship dance was great fun, going off in steam launches to a brightly decorated ship, with plenty of chaperones of course, but as for dancing that was not so nice and I always disliked dancing at sea.

The General commanding the Western District lived at Devonport in Government House at Mount Wise, just opposite the Commander-in-Chief's house, Admiralty House. Sir William Butler was the General in 1899 and I think arrived about the same time that we did. He had been in South Africa and we heard had been re-called because he was not altogether anti-Boer. He was a tall rather fierce looking old man with a white moustache. His wife was the famous artist Lady Butler who painted 'Scotland For Ever', 'The Roll Call' and other pictures of soldiers. She had a clever sweet kind face. We did not see much of her as she was busy in her studio, but she was always very kind and charming to us. They were Roman Catholics, and that also seemed to set the Butlers a little apart. There was a grown up daughter, Coos. who had Irish wit and was graceful and a perfect dancer, and sons, one of whom was studying to be a priest, and a very pretty younger girl at a convent school. One evening at a dance they gave, something was wrong with a suspender and I went to the ladies' room for repairs, and saw leaning against the wall 'Scotland For Ever' so looked and looked at it - and forgot about my partner. Lady Butler said an interesting thing to me when she came for a picnic with us in Father's pinnace. She was looking at the seamen with her artist's eye, and wished that she had seen more of sailors for she would have preferred painting them to soldiers, and showed me what splendid necks and shoulders they have and complained that soldiers' necks were always shut up in collars. She had a great friend, Mrs Collier, who lived in the country near Plymouth and who was also an R.C. Lady Butler chaperoned me to a dance at W... the house where I had spent the cold weekend rehearsing, and asked me to dinner beforehand. It was a Friday, so there was no meat; consider how I felt when served with some game, the only one eating it, while the Butler family waited for their pudding and savoury. I suppose dear Lady Butler - or her housekeeper - thought the heretic would be hungry.

The Fairfaxes were at Admiralty House. He was a distinguished looking old Admiral, and Lady Fairfax a little delicate lady, very thin and fragile looking. She never wore low cut evening dresses, but wore them with net or chiffon tops and soft collars - on which her diamonds looked their sparkling best. In the early spring of 1900 they went to Italy and while driving together one afternoon Sir Henry suddenly died in the carriage. The new Naval Commander-in-Chief was Admiral Lord Charles Scott, a brother of the Duke of Buccleuch. He had a most charming wife (who like Lady Fairfax was very kind to us girls) and two schoolboy sons, the elder at Eton, the younger at Harrow. The Flag Lieutenant to Sir Henry Fairfax stayed on with the new Commander-In-Chief and was Lieutenant the Hon. Lionel Lambart RN, the second son of the Earl of Cavan. The elder son is now Field Marshall Lord Cavan. Mr Lambart retired from the Navy about 1903, had a Command during the 1914 -18 War and won the D.S.O. at the Dardanelles, and went down with his ship at Dunkirk. He was one of the very nicest men I knew as a girl. He was extraordinarily kind to me and I looked up to him and enjoyed talking to him.

Ill with Jaundice

At the time that the Fairfaxes had gone to Italy I was ill first with inflammation of the tummy, a horrid affair, and then with jaundice which was far easier to bear. The first disease lasted a fortnight, and seemed to last a year, as one was continually sick with a splitting headache and pain, and the only thing I was given to eat was a very little milk and soda. I have hated milk and soda ever since! I was better one day, and then the jaundice started. The doctor told me to try and sit up that day and to get up later - or I should be ill for three months. I sat up - next day got up and had my hair brushed and combed and the following day crept downstairs and out of doors and walked 100 yards, where I got stuck and was found by the doctor and marched home. I was a deep orange all over and he was horrified to find me out, but it did no harm. Our doctoring was rather rough and ready. There were two Naval Surgeons in the dockyard and one or other of them doctored us. However we survived it. After that walk I was kept indoors, but came downstairs and slowly got better. Father said I was the least vain person he knew, for no other girl he had met would have appeared in the drawing room with orange face and hands and talked to the young men callers. I didn't care what I looked like, anything was better than feeling sick and having to sip milk and soda. Aunt Carrie wrote and asked if one of us would stay with her as she was alone, and as I had been ill the family said I should go.

Staying with Aunt Connie in south Devonshire in the summer

I went off to Aunt Carrie on a cold March day. She sent her Victoria to the station to meet me. This was a carriage with a seat for two people and a big hood like the hood of a bath chair which could be pulled forward if it rained. It was snowing and nearly dark when I got to Petersfield at last, and drove in the draughty Victoria to the small house where Aunt Carrie was living while alterations were being made to Elmwood. She had not realized that I had been ill and often used to say how she saw the poor child arriving in the snow, creeping slowly up the path, and then found that it had jaundice! I didn't care, it was lovely to be with Aunt and I adored her. She took great care of me and kept her little house warm and comfy. We walked to Elmwood every fine day and while I rested she played billiards and saw the workmen and then we went back to the cottage. My cousin Arthur was her architect and built on several rooms to Elmwood without spoiling the front and old portion of the house, which was originally an old Hampshire farm house. I stayed with Aunt until quite well and then went back to all sorts of delightful doings at Devonport including acting the part of Minnie in 'Sweet Lavender' at the R.M.L.I. theatre in the barracks at Stonehouse. It is a romantic silly old play but we had a good time rehearsing. Minnie is engaged to Clem at the beginning of the play, and he falls in love with his landlady's daughter. Minnie does not mind as Horace fills the gap and after lots of ups and downs it all ends happily. This time I had a large basket of daffodils given to me by the Horace and the family took it quite calmly.

Summer was beginning. Spring comes early in South Devonshire and the wild flowers are lovely. The primroses grow in such quantities and have long stems. We bicycled into the country, or took the train out and bicycled home. The favourite picnics were in the steam launch, and we went to many beautiful places up the rivers and also across to Mount Edgecumbe, which is the property on the Cornish side of

Plymouth Sound belonging to Lord Mount Edgecumbe. He allowed us to land where we liked and picnic on his land. On the Channel side masses of enormous rhododendrons were growing, and in the late spring these were a slope of bright colours growing down to the beach. Lord Mount Edgecumbe was an Earl, and a widower, and as a young man had been chosen by Prince Albert and Queen Victoria as one of the very few young people that the Prince of Wales was allowed to know. His unmarried sister, Lady Ernestine Edgecumbe, lived in a very old and perfect house, Cothele, up the Tamar River, quite a famous old house, I think a dower house. I went once to dinner at Mt Edgecumbe. We went by launch and were driven up to the house which was lighted by quantities of lamps. Lord Vansittart sat next to me and I did not think he had his father's or aunt's charming manners; no doubt he was awfully bored by me. He did not bore me, he was a thrill for he wore a set of links, studs and waistcoat buttons of large precious stones set in diamonds. He really ought to have had shoe buckles to match. Some of the courses were served on silver plates, which were rather scratched and also rather noisy, very marvellous to have of course but my plebeian mind preferred china. There used to be garden parties at Mt Edgecumbe when it was very gay, such beautiful trees and lawns and flowers and an orangery, and all the ladies in light dresses with trailing skirts and trimmed hats and parasols. Other picnics were up the Tamar River, past Pentillie with trees hanging over the water, but first past Saltash and its high railway bridge connecting Devon and Cornwall. Saltash is a very old port and has ancient rights. I somehow connect it with Portugal, and that Portuguese ships pay no harbour dues there. Portugal is 'our oldest ally' so my memory may be correct. On the Devonshire side of the river was Apple-tree Cottage. Isn't that a perfect name for a pretty place? We could get early roses at Apple-tree Cottage. Up and up that winding river to Calstock, another dream place standing above the river on high walls, showers of roses hanging over the walls reflected in the water. Our steam launch could go no further. There were other rivers all flowing into Plymouth Sound and all tidal, of course, so we had to be careful not to run aground. We always towed a skiff so could have rowed ashore if caught by an ebb tide, but luckily this never happened to us. I say that we had to be careful and this was true, for one of the joys of these picnics was that we steered the launch. One of the coxswains was always with us, but after we had learnt to steer the men would leave us alone most of the time. We used to steer the launch for Father when he had to inspect ships lying in the harbour, and used to enjoy coming alongside in proper fashion. There was a great deal of traffic about the Hamoaze but not so much in the Sound. We went out in all weathers, and the more rain and wind there was the more the boats' crew left us while they fugged in their small quarters forward. Steering is very interesting, tides and currents have to be known, and your way about the harbour, rules of the sea, and signals (by pressing a bell) to the engine room. Esmé and Kate and I were never as happy as when Father would ask if we would like to take him in the launch. When we were alongside a ship, we waited in the cabin of the launch. Sometimes we were asked to tea on board HMS *Defiance*, the torpedo school ship, moored up a little river in Cornwall. These tea parties were hilarious, as the ship was full of tricks - magnets to remove hairpins and trifles like that. There was an early gramophone called a phonograph which ground out squeaky music or talking, An X-ray apparatus and wireless. I never could understand how any of these marvels worked. One day a chief Petty officer explained to me up on the top deck, but it was all too complicated. They were experimenting with early wireless and 'talking' twelve miles away, and we heard about Admiral Sir Henry Jackson (no relation), the torpedo specialist and scientist, and Marconi, who were working it all out. The X-ray was more fun and we had our hands photographed.

Brother Charlie gets married

Charlie was married in the beginning of 1900 at Barry, South Wales. He and May had been engaged for some time, and when he found his ship was going to England and he could have some leave, he cabled to arrange the wedding. I could not go as I was rehearsing for 'Dandy Dick' and Father would not hear of me missing rehearsals. He quoted about putting one's hand to the plough and not looking back and I took it to heart as a rule of conduct. Charles and May stayed with us during the honeymoon and we all liked May very much.

Brother Tom's Battleship wrecked but he survives

Tom was on the China station and came back to England that summer after the usual three year commission. He was Commander of a battleship which had been the largest ship to go through the Suez Canal. At the entrance the ship grounded on a sandbank and had to be lightened of her coal and stores and all moveable gear, and finally was jumped off by the officers and ship's company. She got clear just as other ships of the Mediterranean Fleet were arriving to help - among them Harold going to Tom's rescue!! How well I remember that grounding, for at breakfast at school Dr Dawes glanced at the 'Times' and read out a few headlines, including 'Wreck of Battleship'. I asked the name, and heard it was Tom's ship. A very nasty moment! Now Tom was back again, but not in that ship as they transferred in the Mediterranean to (I think) the *Revenge*. We went out to the Sound to meet her, and Tom came down the accommodation ladder and sat with us in the steam launch. Lady Morant was staying with us and was there too.

Brother Harold stays next door in Devonport

Harold was in England as he was now for some time on board HMS *Cambridge*, the gunnery school ship at Devonport, which was anchored in the Hamoaze, exactly in front of our house. We saw a great deal of Harold and knew all his friends on board, all 'gunnery' men. The *Cambridge* was another of the old three decker ships roofed over. I remember some of the names Arthur Vyell Vyvyan (afterwards an Air Marshal) and Cathcart Kemble Lambert and Vincent Molteno, Alex. V. Campbell and the hermit Mr. Maxwell Lefroy who did not like 'society' and told me it was barbaric to dance. We asked him to a young dinner party once knowing that he hated parties but would have to accept the Admiral's initiation. Coey painted name cards for this party. The cards had no names and you had to wander round the table and guess which card belonged to you Mr Lefroy guessed his - a hermit crab coming out of its shell! Mr. Campbell's card was a frog, for he really was rather like one. Mine was a pink cheeked dairy maid, my nickname in the port was C.G. short for 'country girl' (The Musical Comedy 'The Country Girl' was running then in London) which I was not supposed to know, but of course I did know.

Learning how to sail

Father had the use of a nine ton sailing yacht, the *Nita,* as well as the steam launch. We did not often use her, but all learnt something about sailing. There was an old second coxswain who must have been over age but was a good sailor, and he taught us sailing, which is not easy in a crowded harbour with tide, river and wind to consider and perhaps a gay row of destroyers dashing along at top speed - or a big ship taking all the wind out of your sails. At these moments the old coxswain Sanders took charge and told Miss afterwards what she ought to have done. He always could forecast the weather, not the way of the Meteorological office as taught by Professor Bevan at school, but his own way according to the moon, and if the wind was backing and so forth. Before going for a picnic we asked him what the weather would be and he would be right. There were also two or three rowing boats, one of which was towed astern to be used for going ashore if we were landing on a beach. The smallest one, a skiff, was light enough for Kate and me to row, and on fine summer mornings Kate would have me up and dressed by 7 o'clock (she was always an early waker) and at the boat shed trying to drag the skiff into the boat harbour. We each took an oar and pulled about the Hamoaze. We used to salute with our oars held upright when the 8 o'clock signal went and the ensigns were hoisted on board all ships, but that was our only prank. We only had one adventure during these early morning energies, and that ended in safety. There was a slight wind in the dockyard one morning, not enough to make us think about the weather and we pulled up towards Keyham and then across to the Cornish side. Here the wind was much stronger and a nasty choppy sea was getting up and we had to pull against it. A few waves splashed into the boat. I was stroke and did not know how nervous Kate had got until she threw her oar into the boat and said it was no use, we should never make it and should go down. I had got hold of her oar and had started to skull, when a painter was thrown over my shoulder, welcome voices called 'Hang on Miss' and we were rescued by some dockyard men who were rowing across to the yard. Such a relief to be towed and oh, how grateful we were! We got home in time for breakfast, which was always sharp at 8.15 a.m., cold and rather wet but did not have to confess what had happened.

Life in the dockyard at Devonport

You may hear stories of dockyard maties being rough and rude, but we were always treated most politely, and felt quite safe going about the yard. Marian and Father took an interest in the women who worked in the flag factory and the rope factory, and also in the orphanage at Devonport, the 'Female Orphanage' was its dreadful name. The girls wore a strange old-fashioned uniform with bonnets tied on with wide ribbons and Marian, who was a member of the Committee, used to worry about the long hours that the children had to spend sitting on benches learning to sew. There was a waiting list of women wanting work in the Rope Walk, and Marian found that these women (mostly widows) were very badly off and were glad of help. At Christmas time we had a tree which would be decorated and lighted for various parties of women and children. There were toys and bags of sweets for the children, and on a table in the room were parcels of woollen stockings and warm skirts and petticoats.

There was also a society to help sailors' wives called 'The Friendly Union of Sailors' Wives'. Members met once a month (I think) in a room in the dockyard, and had some sort of address or talk and we often got up some little entertainment of music and songs, something amusing if possible like 'The Three Old Maids of Lee' in costume. For this we had masks of old women's faces and grey hair fastened to the backs of our heads and turned round with our backs to the audience while singing the last verse. The audience loved this, and they liked it when we wore sunflower head dresses and sang 'Lazily Lazily Drowsily Drowsily' over a property stage wall. Once a doctor gave a talk about how to feed babies and children and this we knew would not be so much appreciated; in fact while I was handing round cups of tea I heard 'What does he know about babies, he has not had any'. He told them not to give babies bacon and this was just foolishness to them. Marian used to visit some of the women and found one tiny baby being fed on soaked bread. The baby did not live. You must remember that these poor mothers were doing their best, living in horrid small crowded houses in very narrow streets in Devonport, often in an 'ope' which is an alley. Their husbands were away for three years and more, unless they were in the Channel Fleet, and they were living on very small allowances. These crowded houses were sad and we could do nothing to improve them as they were slum property belonging to a rich landlord. The main street of Devonport, Fore Street, which starts at the Dockyard gates, used to be a row of temptations to seamen coming ashore, but had been quite changed for many years by two wonderful women, Miss Wintz and Miss Agnes Weston, who spent their lives in helping sailors. They collected money for 'Sailors' Rests' in each naval port, the one at Devonport being the first block next to the gates. They bought up the public houses in the street and leased them as respectable shops. When I was young Jack Tar was no rollicking drunken sailor, he was a responsible man, probably an expert in engineering, electricity, gunnery, altogether a first class citizen. The Sailors' Rest provided cheap meals and cheap lodging, had recreation rooms, provided lock up boxes for valuables, and also catered for the boys from the training ships - large slabs of good stodgy-looking raisin cake were sold to them for a halfpenny. On Sunday evenings there were services in one of the halls to which Esmé and I sometimes went. We would sit on benches and sing hymns, the men calling out which hymns they wanted, all very cheerful, and later there was a short address and prayer. Esmé said I liked to go so as to share a hymn book with a petty Officer. Father did not mind, he approved of our mixing with our fellow men, and never allowed any nonsense about not knowing naval engineers; in fact he insisted on our asking one naval engineer to our dances. The engineering College was at Keyham yard, and as the captain of the College was a great friend of ours, also his charming wife who often chaperoned us to parties, Esmé and I frequently went there. The senior engineer officer was nice too and keen about games. Esmé and I often went in the morning to play squash with the captain and the engineer (Captain Tizard and Mr Greene) and sometimes played tennis instead, or practised in the nets with the cricket pro. The naval engineers used to be recruited from a different class from the executive officers, and socially it must have been difficult on board ship. Father tried to breach the gap, but I think it was Lord Fisher who cured the sore point with his reforms about entering the Navy. All boys to enter at the same age and the different branches of the service to be decided later. Engineering students used to be much older than naval cadets, about seventeen, I think, and they did not have the same rank or the same uniform. We used to go to their dances and their sports and any official doings. The dances really were different, the young couples walked about arm in arm between dances and the girls wore woolly shawls called 'fascinators' and the chaperones wore sensible high dresses. Of course many engineer officers were very nice as well as being clever and travelled men, and I don't want to make us out snobbish, in fact we were the opposite. None of our friends went to the engineer parties.

Raising money for The Female Orphanage

I have mentioned something about the 'Female Orphanage' Most of the little 'females' being orphans of dockyard workmen. A three day bazaar was held in the Town Hall at which Marian had a lampshade and cushion stall. There were side shows in a smaller hall adjoining and we all worked hard at selling and at the side shows. There were competitions too, hat trimming by men, washing a dirty towel by men etc. for which the entrance was threepence and the small hall was packed when Father entered for the dirty towel competition. Each man had a bucket of water, a piece of soap, towel and clothes peg, and had to peg up his 'washing' when time was up. Father frivolled at it, one of his own boats' crew had the bucket near to him and enjoyed himself splashing his Admiral, and the captain of the yard won with the cleanest towel owing to his wiliness, for he noticed that there was only one black smear on each towel so carefully washed the dirty bit and kept the rest of his towel dry and white. Oh, the stuffiness of that bazaar, it was always crowded, and in the evenings everyone seemed to be eating oranges and the hall smelt of orange peel and humans. But our attempts at charity gave us fun. On Sundays the dockyard used to be really quiet, as the riveters were resting.

The Royal British Female Orphan Asylum, Devonport, was established in a private house on 24 May 1839 by Mrs Tripe, for the orphan daughters of men in the Royal Navy, Royal Marines and Army to maintain, educate and train them to earn their own livelihood. It was supported by voluntary contributions and admitted girls between the ages of 5-12 years. The girls were supported until they were old enough to go into service. In October 1839 Queen Victoria extended her patronage and the institution formally became the Royal British Female Orphan Asylum. A house in St Michael's Terrace, Stoke, was rented from May 1840 and by 1845 the foundation stone was laid of a large orphanage building in Albert Road. Two wings were added in 1874 to accommodate 50 children to be supported by the Admiralty, raising the accommodation to 200 children, with a further enlargement made in 1892. During 1906 the home changed its name to the Royal United Services Orphan Home for Girls.

Church in the dockyard

The men electrically riveting the plates of a new ship and the men in the boiler house made the most noise. The latter was deafening as they worked in a shed. But everything was noisy, and on Sundays there was almost a hush only broken by the Chapel bells. Dockyards have their own 'chapels' which are churches with a naval chaplain in charge. The one at Devonport was near the gates, up the cobbled path past the old figureheads, near the expense accounts offices where the men were paid. The chapel was large and ugly, with a rounded apse, and galleries where the ships' companies sat. The walls were painted, and there was a huge pulpit as big as a 'three decker'. It may have been a converted three decker? The Ten Commandments in elegant print hung on each side of the altar, and the whole church was solid and 18th century and looked more like a hall than a church. There was a vestry for the chaplain on the north side and one for the Admirals on the south - our vestry was a little room, with a table covered with a purple red cover, a purple red carpet and hat pegs. We left umbrellas and water proofs and uniform caps there, and also had a chat with the Commander-in-Chief's party. He had the two front pews on the north side, and we had the two front pews on the south side. Dockyard officials all had their pews, all in order of importance! Officers from ships in dock or in port also sat on the ground floor (it really was like a hall). Upstairs were the seamen and marines, sometimes a great many of them. And how splendidly they sang. They took possession of the singing when they liked a hymn, and their singing was the part I liked best of the service. They used almost to shout especial favourites such as

'Crown Him with Many Crowns' and 'Their Spirits Longed and Fainted' at the top of their voices.

A dog called Joe

Those morning services remind me of Father's dog Joe, a fox terrier who was a mighty hunter of rats. He escorted Father to church and was waiting when we came out to go for our Sunday walk. This was a walk about the yard, hoping that Joe would find some rats, and he always did. He went everywhere with Father, and went on board ships when they were inspected before sailing. Once he smelt a rat on board a ship that was just due to leave, in a place where there was no crack or possible place that a rat could be. Father knew that if Joe smelt rat there <u>was</u> a rat, and had the place opened up and thus delayed the ship - and Joe was right. Everyone knew Joe who was a cheerful friendly well behaved dog as well as such a clever one - even King Edward VII had heard of him.

Dinner parties

It is no wonder that on looking back to those years in the Dockyard I remember a great many dinner parties, for not only did I write the invitations and name cards and decide on who should take in who, but I was very often at the dinner, and always in the drawing room afterwards, as I had to play. We had to entertain all the naval and military grandees, dockyard officials, and return hospitality, and also if a foreign ship were in port we gave a dinner party for the Captain and staff. My first dinner party was one given when a Danish ship had come in. The officers of a German ship were interested in our music, and wanted to sit by the piano and be absorbed by it, instead of sitting at the other end of the room talking to Marian and Father - who thought they were just sentimental Germans full of *sehnsucht*. A Chilean cruiser was more interesting and we liked the cheerful officers, many of whom had Scotch surnames, spoke good English and copied our navy. (During the 1914-18 War a Chilean cruiser came to Wellington, and Norton and I were asked to a tea party that Lord and Lady Liverpool gave for the officers. Nobody could remember if Chile was an ally, or pro-ally, or pro-German, and nobody liked to ask the guests for that would look as if they were not very important. It turned out that the Chilean Navy was pro-ally and their Army pro-German and the Government neutral – See Book II). I was staying at Elmwood while this Chilean ship was still in English waters, and after I had left a wire came from one of our Chilean friends asking me on board at Spithead. Aunt and Uncle George got rather unnecessarily upset, for I would not go on board South American ships because I was scared of them. An extraordinary Brazilian ship came to Devonport and had to go into dock and I kept well away from her for the following reason.

Beware of Brazilians

The Commander-in-Chief, Lord Charles Scott, gave a dinner for the Brazilian officers and we were asked too. Father, Kate and I went. Father sat by Lady Charles, Lord Charles took me in; Kate had a black bearded Brazilian captain. We all spoke French all the evening as the guests knew French but not English. I was wearing a couple of red roses on my white evening dress, and during dinner I knocked them or something and they fell down. Kate's bearded captain jumped up, came round the table, picked up the roses, went back to his seat and then presented them to me with a low bow over the table. After dinner he started talking to me and said I was his fate, and had I ever looked at the stars and wondered which my star was, and I was his star - and a proposal! I fled to the flag lieutenant and told him not to leave me for a second as I was afraid of Brazilians. Driving home of course Father had to have his laugh about the rose incident - and I told him of the proposal. How he shouted with laughter 'Did you say you were not going to marry a black monkey?' Before leaving the port the Brazilians gave an At Home on board to which I refused to go, which amused Father again. But I really was frightened of them although it seemed funny afterwards.

Gallant Russians

A Russian ship, a new battleship the *Petropavlovsk* came on her way to Vladivostok - or was it Port Arthur then? The Russian Captain often sat in our drawing room; he always wore white cotton gloves and was quiet and shy. We had all been asked to see his ship and went out one morning to where she was anchored in the Sound near the breakwater. The young Russian officers were rather thrilled that the steam launch was steered by a girl. We all went, and Aunt Nora too. Directly we got on board we were each given large bridesmaids' bouquets which we had to hold all the time we were there. I said that mine was the prettiest - it was large dusty pink chrysanthemums with small bunches of Parma violets in between them, a lovely mixture of colours. We walked about the quarter deck conducted by lots of officers and then asked to go below and see some more of the ship. The crew and the crew's quarters did not seem to be quite so grand a spectacle. Then we went to the wardroom and there given Sweet Champagne. Aunt Nora was thrilled to bits with her bouquet and her cluster of officers and when she saw the Champagne asked what it was because she did not drink wine. The Russians said it was lemonade, so Aunt Nora drank it down, although a bit suspicious. It was no treat to drink in the morning we thought, and we were all headachy and tired when we got home with our bouquets and our ship's cap ribbons tied round our arms. I think I still have that ribbon with NETPONAV...K in Russian letters. Poor ship, she was blown up in the Russian Japanese War and nearly everyone on board was killed, one of the few to escape being the Grand Duke Cyril of Russia, then a young man. After the Czar and

Czarevitch were murdered he was heir to the Russian throne. He is dead now and so is his wife, Tem's Princess Victoria of Edinburgh.

Jackson cousins

During the summer holidays of 1900 we had some children to stay with us; our cousin Reggie and Molly Jackson, Nanette Murray and her Mother, and Gwen Hanbury Davies who was Marian's godchild. Tom was having leave, and Harold was often ashore, and Father, Kate and I were at home. Reggie was a charming boy about twelve, and Molly a dear good little girl three years younger, Nanette was a graceful bright slip of a girl of sixteen and Gwen the 'bright little thing' she hates to be called but always will be. We were such a happy party and Mrs Murray was as cheerful as any. She was very stout and told funny stories. We played all sorts of games. Tom and Nanette made real friends and used to throw a ball to each other by the hour, until Father got annoyed. Reggie wanted to go into the Navy so he was blissful among all the ships, and as he had such perfect manners our friends liked to have him on board. Molly held herself bolt upright, never was there such a straight back and to 'Molly' meant 'Hold yourself up'. She slept in my room and one day did not want to get up. I knew nothing of illness and thought she was tired; she just lay quietly all day and then was quite well. It was only after her tragic death that we knew she must have been in pain that day. She went to a boarding school and concealed her pains there, too, for fear of worrying Aunt Robin and Uncle Fred. She had acute appendicitis and it was too late for the doctors to save her life. She was going to see the Coronation procession with her godmother Lady Northcliffe and Aunt Robin had made her a pretty white frock for this, and poor little unselfish Molly was buried in it instead. This was in May 1902. We all loved her for she was a cheerful smiling child and her death was a great shock; imagine what it was like for her parents. Reggie did not enter the Navy after all. In 1914 he was in the Army in France, was shot through both legs and was back in France three months later. He spoke perfect French and was a liaison officer, had the Légion d' Honneur and after the War lived in Paris for some years where he was in business. He died in 1937 aged fifty; his heart was worn out during those years in France at the War. He always was charming, and good and kind too. Gwen went to the convent school kept by the Clewer Sisters, a Church of England Sisterhood. She and I became great friends although she was six years younger, and this friendship has lasted for forty years. She is Mrs Farleigh Greig and lives at Fleet in Hampshire now and has a son in the Army. Before she was married she lived In Sydney with her father, who had a Government position there, and stayed with us two summers at Hiwiroa. She is one of Jocelyn's godmothers.

Launching Ships

Of course the greatest excitement in a dockyard is the launch of a big ship, and while we were living in the yard some battleships were launched. We watched all the preparations, and were on the launching platform when the great moment arrived when HMS *Bulwark, Implacable* and *Queen* were named, dog-shores knocked away - a few seconds of waiting – 'Will she move?' - a tiny movement - a roar of cheering from the thousands of dockyard men and the ship slides at great speed into the water. It is really thrilling and makes one shout and cheer and laugh. Nowadays one can see a launch at the cinema, but one does not get that same thrill. If you have seen a ship built, prepared for launching, and heard the solemn service and waited for what seems like minutes, but in my experience was only seconds, for the big ship to slide backwards down the sloping blocks, when she is safely in the water it seems a triumph. She is sometimes helped on her way by hydraulic rams. There is an awful feeling (at least I had it) that she might topple over on her side. The royal yacht, *Victoria and Albert* turned over after launching which was a ghastly thing for the chief constructor and his staff - but due, so we were told, to too many royal instructions from Queen Victoria so that the ship was top heavy before launching.

Life after Queen Victoria

Queen Victoria died in January 1901. People had got used to the South African war, the worst of it was over, only the endless rounding up continued until Peace in June 1902, and so in Naval and Military places life was cheerful and we were allowed to dance and have parties. Regiments had gone to South Africa, but barracks were filled by militia. Queen Victoria was old, and I felt no sorrow about her, but she was the end of a period, and older people wept and wondered what would happen now. There was a tremendous 'do' over her funeral, a real Victorian affair! Father knew a day or two before that she was dying, and told us to get ready as we should have to wear black, so we took some clothes to be dyed. There was a dance in the country the evening she died and we did hope to get to it. The carriage was at the door when the telephone message came to Father that she had gone, and he would not let us start. Everyone else went to the dance, and heard about the Queen after they had started the party. The band went home, and the dance fizzled out. Next morning everyone was in black, and the streets decorated with purple and black - and the new King Edward VII proclaimed. It was a great change for all the middle-aged and older people, since 1837 there had been Queen Victoria. Prayers had to be altered; they could not even sing 'God Save the Queen' any longer. She was buried at Windsor ten days later, taken from the Isle of Wight in her funny old yacht to Portsmouth, and next day in a great procession across London, and then by train to Windsor - but I did not see any of this. Tom told us that he was much impressed by the playing of Chopin's funeral March and by the marching of the seamen who marched with bent heads. We went to a funeral service in the Dockyard Chapel. All those ten days every blind in our house was pulled down and everything seemed very gloomy. After we had been to the service Kate and I went up to the top of the house to the signal room to watch through the windows the firing of the 101 guns of the Royal Salute. While we were there we felt the reaction to all the funeral talks and sights, and we laughed and made a noise (nobody could hear us) and when a gunner made some especially good smoke rings we cheered. I think these rings are made by greasing the mouth of the gun; anyway making rings must have varied the monotony for the gunners. We had to wear deep mourning for three months, and half mourning for another three. General mourning was only half this length of time, but we were official mourners living in a Royal Dockyard. Black suited Esmé and me as we were fair, but it did not suit Kate who had a brown complexion. She wore a narrow line of white in her collar and was scolded for this by Father. After six weeks I was in London and everyone there was wearing large bunches of violets, particularly Parma violets, which looked so gay to me, but of course I could not wear any. Everyone was in black for the Queen, poor and rich and I expect it would have pleased her.

It must have been before her death that we had a fancy dress dance. Marian was dressed as 'Canada' (she was a Canadian) and we three were dressed alike as White Pierrettes. The short skirts were very comfortable to dance in, and the ruffles were very hot. Two of our guests were unrecognised, an R.A. Major who came as an old bent peddler, and an R.E. Captain, a very shy man, was a rag doll. I knew the peddler but then I was rehearsing with him at the time so could see through the disguise. The R.E. Captain had dressed in a quiet corner of the Dockyard near our house - and after an hour or two he went away and came back in his uniform, very beautiful and correct in scarlet and gold tunic. Marian scolded him for coming late! What fun it all was.

Father's friend, Prince Louis of Battenberg was at the Admiralty (Naval Intelligence I think he was), and also Admiral Sir Arthur K. Wilson, who was Comptroller, who had been Father's great friend on board the *Calcutta* when they were Naval Cadets. Both these used to come to see us.

Prince Louis of Battenberg

Four months after the Queen's death we were going to a wedding. We finished our lunch quickly and then dressed. Prince Louis and Father had lunch later, and when I was ready I went to the dining room to see Prince Louis whom I thought the most beautiful and thrilling person. I wore a new pale grey dress and black hat. Father at once said I was too gaily dressed, and appealed to Prince Louis who said 'I think she looks very nice'. Then Esmé came in, in a black coat and skirt and light blouse 'That is Better' said Father. Then arrived Marian, in a bright red dress and red hat, very cheerfully saying 'It is unlucky to wear mourning at a wedding'. Wasn't that funny? Both men struck dumb! Prince Louis was tall and slim and very handsome, younger than Father and I thought him perfect! He was a Serene Highness, not an H.R.H., and had married Princess Louise, a granddaughter of Queen Victoria's. His brother, Henry, had married the Queen's youngest child, Princess Beatrice, and was dead. He had died during the Benin Expedition in West Africa and evil gossip said he wanted to die because living at Windsor or Osborne with the Queen was a deadly dull life for a man. Queen Victoria would not let Princess Beatrice leave her. Prince Louis had always been in our Navy and was a very clever officer.

Whisky in the piano!

Once when he and Father were in the Mediterranean Squadron they were rehearsing for a musical play. The Commander-in-Chief, the Duke of Edinburgh, lent his big cabin for a rehearsal one evening that he was dining ashore. When drinks came at the end of the evening, one of the cheerful actors said 'Poor piano has been working hard and must have a drink and poured a whisky and soda into the Duke's piano! Who did it, Father or Prince Louis? If I asked Father he would say 'Ask Prince Louis', or ask Prince Louis and he would say 'Your father will tell you'. I never heard what the Duke said. He was very musical and must have discovered the damage. Once Father said that it wasn't the Duke's best piano.

Lord Roberts came to Plymouth on an inspection tour, and in the evening Sir William and Lady Butler gave a reception for him and Father took me to it. I was lucky, as only Naval and Military grandees were there. Prince Louis was there and Naval officers wore 'ball dress', which means epaulettes and quantities of gold lace. He and I had a long talk, at least he did the talking and I sat and admired. Lord Roberts had General (or was he Field Marshal then?) Sir Evelyn Wood with him, and I talked with him too, and also with Lord Roberts' very tall A.D.C. Captain Dawnay, who told me that Lord Roberts was a dear. At the end of the evening Lady Butler introduced me to the great little man. He really was quite small, and so was Sir Evelyn Wood. He had great charm - and uneven discoloured teeth. He asked me why Father had not been with him during his inspection of forts that morning and I, as usual saying the first thing that came into my head, said "Oh, but he's a very <u>busy</u> man' - Lord Roberts laughed and all was well. I was so proud to meet him. It was a red star in my life. He seemed so good and kind, and someone you would do anything for. No wonder everyone loved 'Bobs'. I was the only girl at the party except Lady Butler's daughter, so was <u>very</u> lucky.

Lord Roberts enters the city of Kimberley after the relief of the besieged city in 1900

A new Battleship and Relations

Later Prince Louis commissioned a new battleship, the *Implacable,* to go to the Mediterranean Squadron. The Sunday she sailed he asked Lord and Lady Charles Scott and me to lunch on board. I went in our steam launch in our coxswain Brebner's care, and Lady C.S. was my chaperone. When we were leaving, the Commander-in-Chief's barge naturally came alongside before Father's and the Scotts left before me. So for a few minutes I was the only woman on board, and how the officers teased me. 'What shall you do if I give orders to up anchor and sail?' said Prince Louis, seeing me off. That was the last I saw of him, and a nice memory. He was First Lord when the 1914 War started, and retired because of being of German birth. His wife's sister was the Czarina, and he was fond of her, and told me about her. She gave him bell pushes for his cabin in his new ship, made of precious stones. He was not well off, and had a family to bring up. I am glad to have known some outstandingly nice men when I was young, men of brains and charm and good manners. He was one, Admiral John Denison, my Uncles Blomfield and Fred, and some fine good young officers in the Navy and Army.

We often had relations staying with us, and Helen used to come with her little boy Geoffrey, as Clifford was in South Africa. Every week she used to send him a small parcel by letter post which contained 6 pairs of new socks, a handkerchief and a few lumps of sugar for his charger. She always darned the heels of the socks so as to make them wear better. We used to hear that parcels did not reach the troops as there was such congestion at Cape Town, and when Norton and I were at Cape Town In 1913 we could understand this, as the harbour seemed so small and the wharves so few to supply an Army of a quarter of a million men.

One of our Cruisers, HMS *Doris,* came back from South Africa and her officers were given a dinner by the port officers - Father was in the chair, and no newspaper correspondents were allowed so that the after dinner speakers were free to say what they thought. The dinner was at the Devonport hotel which had a small gallery for musicians in the big dining room. This gallery was draped with flags, and we were allowed to crawl in on our hands and knees and listen to the speeches. Father's introductory remarks were that he was not going to speak except to say that 'We would all have given our eyes to be there'. They talked about Ladysmith and Naval guns etc., but even now I am not going to say more, as we promised not to say anything of what we heard. By the way, the *Doris* was pronounced with the long Greek Omega <u>*Dooris*</u> which Father always used. He thought it illiterate to say '*Dorris*'.

The visit of King Edward VII with Alexandra to launch *The Queen*

HMS Queen

One of the greatest excitements during our life in the Dockyard was when King Edward VII and Queen Alexandra came to launch the battleship *Queen.* The King laid the foundation stone of the new barracks for naval cadets at Dartmouth, and then came to Devonport and stayed in the dockyard on board the new yacht the *Victoria and Albert* which lay alongside the quay exactly opposite our house at the bottom of the steps. It was March 1902, which is full spring in South Devon, and I think it was almost the first cheerful event that the Royal family had had since they were plunged into the deepest mourning by the old Queen's death. Devonport was excited, the dockyard men happy, and the weather warm and calm. Fore Street, Devonport, which leads to the Dockyard Gates, was turned into a bower of roses - hundreds of strings of paper roses were hung high above and across the street from house to house.

Uncle Blomfield stayed with us and so did Admiral Sir Edward Seymour - another handsome courtier-like man to whom of course I lost my heart once more, and also Tom who was at the Admiralty. Tom was then Assistant Director of Naval Intelligence. We stood on the top of the steps to watch the Royalties drive past to the yacht, and they at once recognised Uncle Blomfield and waved to him. Princess Victoria was with them, and Uncle Blomfield had been her tutor so no wonder they were pleased to see an old friend's face. He had dinner on board with them one evening and Sir Edward another evening and Father too. When we first heard that Queen Alexandra was coming to launch the *Queen* I suggested that the King should lay the first keel plate of the next new battleship. Impossible said Father. I told the Chief Constructor, Mr Champness, whose answer was the same, but I kept on and on, telling him that he was missing a great opportunity, <u>why</u> couldn't some arrangement be made that the keel plate was ready and slid onto the building slip when the *Queen* was in the Hamoaze? Couldn't the King press a button or something to move the keel plate into place? Think how pleased this would make him? I would not let it drop. Mr Champness finally saw the idea - and it was done! He received lots of credit for it. I did not want any credit, I just wanted it to happen and have always had the comfortable feeling that I did do something once in the Dockyard world. Chatham Dockyard followed suit at their next big launching.

As well as the launch, the King had come to present the China medals to the Naval brigade who had marched to the relief of the Legations at Peking, The medals were given on the big parade ground at Keyham dockyard, which is part of Devonport yard, separated from it by part of Devonport town and the ferry landing from Tor Point in Cornwall, but joined by a tunnel through which there is a railway line. The Royal party went to Keyham yard in the train, and Tom travelled in the engine! It was a very good 'show' but there was no sunshine. I had a very good view as I was standing by the Duchess of Buccleuch's chair. She was the Mistress of the Robes and a very great and dignified lady. The Duke was there too; they were staying with his brother, Admiral Lord Charles Scott. They were the Duchess of Gloucester's grandparents. As far as I can remember her parents were there too, slim sweet looking young people, interested in the dockyard. Sir Edward Seymour (who was staying with us) had been Commander in Chief of the Naval Brigade, so was with those who were being honoured by the King. There was a short thin Naval Captain called Jellicoe 'Very clever young man, quite a coming man'. This Captain Jellicoe was married to, or was marrying, an heiress, and another 'coming man' called Madden was married to her sister, daughter of a Mr Cayzer. There was a brother of theirs in the Navy, very well off, who used to call on us. I did not care for him; he fidgeted his feet when he was sitting!

Marian was just behind Queen Alexandra during the medal giving, and said that she wore a long black corded silk coat which had been let out down the seams! The Queen wore a black sequin dress for the launching ceremony, like a high long sleeved evening dress. It suited her perfect figure. She wore a toque on top of her curled brown fringe. The launch was in the afternoon and was a tremendous success, everything went off perfectly. I cannot describe the excitement, all the workmen and foremen and officers so keyed up to make everything perfect for the King and Queen. We were with the Royalties on the launching platform. Queen Alexandra got bright rosy pink with excitement when the big ship moved, so don't listen when people tell you that her face was coated with <u>enamel</u>. She really was lovely with even features, clear skin, hazel eyes with tiny wrinkles round them, a long slender neck and a slim figure with all the curves perfect. She was very deaf and had a stiff knee. I don't know if her hair grew on her head but anyway it matched her complexion and did not look like a wig. The deafness must have made her rather lonely and shy. She liked to have a camera handy and take dozens of snapshots.

The King was stout but held himself so well that he looked taller than he was. He had to have a very long naval belt to go round his waist! Disappointingly the gold lace was rather tarnished. Father started cheering when the ship moved, and the cinema man caught him - and If you wanted to you could go to the Polytechnic in Regent Street to see the launching of HMS *Queen* and the inside of Father's mouth! I saw Harold once at the Polytechnic during a showing of South African War films, in 'our gallant seamen at the front dragging a famous 4.7 gun'. It was Harold with a gun crew practising at Whale Island near Portsmouth. How we laughed and clapped our gallant seamen. I must go back to the launch. I am a first class wanderer from the subject. After HMS *Queen* was safely in the Hamoaze the King pressed an electric switch on the launching platform, and the first keel plate of the next new battleship, to be named after him, slid from the right into its place in the centre of the slipway and the King said 'I declare this plate well and "trhuly" laid'. He always said German R's but otherwise had no German accent. He so often laid foundation stones 'well and trhuly' and his German R was a joke. Did Victoria speak English with a German accent? I expect she did as German was her Mother tongue. King Edward VII spoke German, so we were told, with an English accent, but his French was perfect. If he could roll his R's it is a pity he did not always, as so many English people do (my brother Harold for example). After the launching ceremony the Royal party drove back to the yacht, and we hurried home.

An awning had been put up from our front door to the road. Marian had a colour scheme for this and the house decorations, all of yellows and golds with some tawny brown in the awning. The drawing room was yellow gold and tawny red - so it all blended. The staircase had masses of yellow daffodils which brightened it up. We heard that the Queen admired it all, a change from red-white-and-blue and from the Admiralty's purple red carpets. The King and Queen and Princess Victoria and their suite all came to tea with us, and about eighty of the leading people of the Port and of Devonshire were invited. The eighty arrived at the house immediately after the launch and went to the dining room, where tea was served. Marian had gone upstairs and taken Esmé and Kate with her to put final touches to the flowers and to the tea table in the back drawing room (you will remember that the drawing room took up all the first floor). This left Tom and me to receive our important guests, and they really were important and I longed for Esmé and Kate to share the fun. Tom was simply marvellous with them and so was Sir Edward Seymour. I stood at the door of the dining room and received them. The Duke and Duchess of Buccleuch and Lady Constance Scott, their daughter, the High Sheriff, Miss Agnes Weston, who was quite sure the Royalties would want to meet her. Poor dear, they did not ask for her to go to the drawing room. I hope she was not dreadfully disappointed. Tom, who had been in Japan, was delegated to look after a group of very small and deeply bowing Japanese Naval officers. A delegation sent by the Kaiser of German Naval officers, very tall; the Chief Admiral, a Graf Von Arnim, in his beautiful uniform with white revers. Then a little sweet faced lady saying 'You don't know me my dear but I'm little Mrs Wigans of Clovelly Court' It was all just too wonderful. Then Tom said to me that it was nearly time for the King and Queen to arrive so I slipped into the hall to make sure that nobody was there, for it had been ordered that no one was to be there or on the staircase when they came, so that the Queen could go upstairs quietly. Her stiff knee made this awkward for her. In the hall I saw a <u>very</u> nice-looking lady and asked her if she would mind coming into the dining room as the King and Queen did not want anyone but my parents there when they arrived. She smiled and said it was all right for she was Lady Aislie and was in attendance on Her Majesty. She was so sweet and smiling that I did not feel a bit that I had done the wrong thing. The Royalties arrived, went up to the drawing room and asked for the family, so Tom and Uncle Blomfield and I went to them. They did not want any servants in the room with the tea - so there was a good sized table in the back drawing room and behind this table was Miss Cregoe, Rose's governess, looking after the teapots. There was a smaller table just in the big drawing room, with plates of small cakes and biscuits and various kinds of sandwiches. The King drank 'Russian' tea, that is tea in a tumbler with slices of lemon in it. The Queen asked if she might pour out her own, and went to the back drawing room and had a short talk to the delighted Miss Cregoe. Marian gave the King his tumbler and I handed him sandwiches. The Royalties walked about and took what they wanted to eat. They signed their photographs for Marian. Admiral Sir Hedworth Lambton was there (afterwards Lord Meux), very cheerful, suggesting to Miss Charlotte Knollys and me that we should dance a breakdown to cheer things up. 'Hedworth', as they called him, was great fun. Miss Knollys was the Queen's devoted friend. She was shortish and plain and nice and everyone knew what a comfort she was to the beautiful deaf Queen. When the King spoke to his wife he put his hand on her shoulder and talked loudly in her ear. The Buccleuch's were sent for from downstairs, and I shall never forget the low curtsies that the Duchess and her daughter made to the King and Queen. Lady Constance was wearing a brown dress with a full skirt and made the loveliest curtsey. Princess Victoria said 'Hallo Connie' to her. Princess Victoria was like the Queen but taller, not so pretty and <u>very</u> slim. She and Uncle Blomfield and Tom had foregathered. She told Tom that Uncle Blomfield had been her tutor and Tom said 'He once tried to teach me to read, but he failed'. She said that Uncle Blomfield's favourite was Louise. Louise could do nothing wrong, but it was Louise who sawed the back off the chair. (Louise was H.H.H. the Duchess of Fife). The story is that the three Wales Princesses were not quite the perfect little darlings Uncle Blomfield thought they were. One day, Louise sawed the back of his chair nearly off, so that when he leaned back it broke off, and he thought he had broken a Marlborough House chair and was very upset about it, and apologized humbly to the Princess of Wales when she came in. And all those years he thought he had broken the chair!

The King and Queen then did a very kind thing. They said they wanted Esmé, Kate and me presented to them. Sir Hedworth Lambton led us to the King and we curtseyed in a row - and then to the Queen. It was a formal presentation (to Court as a Court presentation) with everyone at attention. Poor Kate, when she curtseyed to the Queen, her stiff right knee misbehaved and she knocked over a tiny table - it had nothing on it, and nobody paid any attention, but afterwards the family yarn was that Kate upset the tea table! After our curtseys to the Queen she talked to us three, standing by one of the long windows looking out at the sunset with a strong light on her face, so I could see there was no enamel. She talked about dancing, and that she had heard the drawing room had a good floor for dancing, and things like that. We smiled and agreed, and one could not talk to her as she could not hear. Then they left, and Marian kissed the King's hand as he got into his carriage. I don't think he enjoyed hand kissing but she had said she was determined to do it. I nearly forgot about Rose and the cigarettes. She was to hand round the cigarette box after tea and did this very nicely. The King refused, and she turned round and walked back to Marian at the other end of the room saying in her clear child's voice 'He doesn't want any'. Everyone smiled and laughed and the King was amused. When the Royal party had gone, the grandees in the diningroom left - and the Jackson family assembled in the drawingroom, tired but feeling Oh, what a wonderful day. I sat on the floor at Sir Edward Seymour's feet, holding his cocked hat and feeling quite blissful. But the greatest thrill of all was to come.

A Knighthood in the bedroom

Father had been asked to dinner on board the Royal Yacht that evening. Marian was not invited because she had not been to court since her wedding. Poor Marian, wasn't that bad luck. When Father got on board one of the naval equerries (Capt. Egerton) said to him that His Majesty wanted to see him in his room, and took him there. The King said 'I'm going to knight you, kneel down' and then and there knighted him. 'Rise, Sir Thomas etc', and hung the Order of K.C.V.O. round his neck. 'That ribbon is a mile too long, go to my dressing room and my Valet will put it right'. The ribbon was shortened and Father was taken off to dinner, feeling completely dazed. He told us he felt so taken aback as if he were drunk. The Queen bowed and smiled to him and touched her neck where his Order was hanging to show her pleasure with his decoration. The Victorian Order was then (I don't know about nowadays) the only Order entirely in the King's hands, which he could give to his friends and people whom he wanted to honour. Other Orders were political, War Office and Admiralty recommendations. The King was so pleased with all the arrangements that Father had made, and thanked him in the most wonderful way by being knighted on board ship by the King's own wish. Tom was sitting up for Father so was the first to congratulate him, and we were all very pleased and excited next day. Marian was now my lady and your ladyship and the maids liked saying it. Father's name was Sturges. He had never been called Thomas, but he decided on being Sir Thomas and not Sir Sturges, as the latter was supposed to be difficult to say. His relations always called him Sturgie. The Royalties went to church in the Dockyard Chapel, and at the end of the service while God Save the King was being sung, they left the church. I remember that they went about the harbour and to Mount Edgecumbe, and the Queen was busy with her camera. It must have been a little holiday for them, and we heard that the King liked being protected by his Navy for a change. He came to Devonport again before we left, just a short visit. He was driving to Mount Wise as we came out of church that Sunday. There was a high wind and my hat blew off, and as I ran after it he leaned out of the carriage window and waved his top hat!

Brothers, nieces and nephews

During these years at Devonport Charlie and May were married and stayed with us during their honeymoon. Harold and Louie Browne were engaged; Harold left the gunnery ship HMS *Cambridge* and went to the Mediterranean. Tom came back from the China Station and was at the Admiralty and Esther and Hugh were still living at Penzance. Clifford was in South Africa. Little nephews and a small niece used to come and stay. Tom Evans, who was very clever and could read the newspaper to us when he was five, and was always interested in what he called the 'leckerlek' (electric) trams. Geoffrey Coffin, a pretty little boy who never said anything but a few baby words; Bobby Evans, dark and good looking and naughty and most lovable. He arrived one Sunday afternoon, stood in front of the fire in his sailor clothes, looked at us all and said 'Did you put on those pretty blouses because you knew I was coming?' He slept in my room, and used to want me to play tigers with him at 5 a.m.! I had him out for a walk once and he lay in the gutter in Fore Street and refused to move. At last I said I was going to fetch a policeman from the Dockyard Gate - and that awful threat got him up in a moment. He was only four. Dear Bobby, always friendly and satisfied, he even had a very dirty tramp for one of his great friends when he was a schoolboy. He was killed at the Battle of Bullecourt fighting with the Australians when he was nineteen. The little niece was Nelly Evans, my godchild. She was a funny little thing with large eyes, rather like a little wild kitten. I am sure she was a child who would have been happier as an only child. Marian was always very kind and patient to Nelly. She and Bobby were great friends. Once when taking

Tom, Bobby and Nelly for a walk I heard Nelly say 'I shall marry you Lobert when I am grown up.' 'What nonsense' (from Tom aged 6) 'You have to marry a complete stranger'.

Several, of our relations and Marian's relations stayed with us. A friend of Esmé's came and I liked her very much. She was Nell Clark, only child of General Sir Andrew Clark, Agent General for Victoria. He was once Governor of the Straits Settlements and it was <u>his</u> idea to call Queen Victoria Empress of India. He was an old War Office friend of Father's. Nell's Mother had died when she was a child and she was an heiress and had her Mother's jewellery. She brought her pearl necklace and diamond necklace, which was a string of big diamonds, with her when she stayed with us. I found poor Nell wearing the diamonds in bed to keep them safe. She must have been glad to get them back into the Bank.

Maud runs away from a kiss

Father was now a Vice Admiral. That means more pay, and a different flag. Rear Admirals' flags have two red pills on the St George's Cross, Vice Admirals have one red pill, and Admirals have the plain red and white cross. I have said how stupid and backward I was about many things. My eyes were always open to colours, and my ear to sounds, but I led a selfish life and in many ways had not grown up. Nobody ever told me anything about what is called 'life' now. I knew absolutely nothing about all that. I thought people only kissed when they were very fond of each other or engaged. I got a shock the first time a man tried to kiss me. I ran away, and as it was at a dance at Lady Butler's at Mount Wise, and in the garden with a full moon, can you imagine anything sillier? I was twenty then. The man got his kiss and I got my surprise. I thought Admiral Sir Roger Keyes a horrible man because he said he wished I were a widow as then he could kiss me. I still think him horrid although he is so famous and such a hero. Also he would drink whisky and soda at our dance instead of the claret cup which satisfied everyone else. Esmé told me once that I was pretty. I was certainly very ignorant - and often in a brown study.

In debt

Then I did a very wrong thing - I over-spent my allowance and got into debt. It was a wicked thing to do. Father gave me £40 a year to dress on and for pocket money. Nobody gave me any advice how to budget on that and that is the only excuse I shall make. I was completely wrong and knew it and deserved a good punishment. Father was very kind about it and took all the bills. I told him I would keep myself until it was all paid off, and I did this and more. Part of my punishment is to write about it now, but it is right that I should, and warn you of the evil of debt. It is a dreadful thing, such a weight on your mind. I told Norton when we were first married. So now you know why I am always in a fuss to get bills paid. Well the first thing to do was to get some employment. I should have liked to go on the stage, but as I used to get bad colds and coughs easily and the back stage is so draughty, I thought twice about it. It is a very uncertain life at best, and also Mrs Henry Head, Cousin Hester's Mother, gave me a message from Sir Cyril Maude <u>not</u> to attempt it. Thanks to Dr Dawes' for sending me in for Exams. I could be a governess, so got in touch with a Governess Agency and heard of a post in Leicestershire. A personal interview was needed, so I packed up and left Devonport for good in a hurry, writing Goodbye letters to my friends in the train on the way to London. Great Western trains were smooth not like New Zealand bone rattlers.

Maud becomes a governess

I stayed at Meck with Uncle Blomfield and Aunt Bessy, and Dolly went with me for the interview, which was at the Conservative Rooms in (I think) Great College? Street, Westminster. A tall middle-aged man received us in an office, rather breathless, but looked prosperous and respectable. His letter had said that he wanted a governess for two girls, aged twelve and fourteen, and that he lived in a new house near Leicester which had electric light. We wondered why his wife did not write to me, but apparently he did all the correspondence. He offered a salary of £50 a year. I said at £50 for the first six months, after that at £60 a year, and he agreed. His letter had mentioned a fortnight's holiday and 'the usual Bank holidays'. It all sounded rather different to anything I had heard of, but I agreed to go. They did not want me until the beginning of August and this was May. We found out from the Travellers' Aid Society that these people were respectable, had recently moved, and attended the Village Church. All my friends teased and laughed and said I would never stick it out, which made me determined to put up with anything sooner than do that. Several people were very kind to me. Nell Clark at once asked me to stay with her in her big house at Portland Place. Her father, General Sir Andrew Clark, had died recently and the house was for sale, the servants gone, so it was gloomy for her to be there while she sorted her father's papers and things. She had a chaperone and a maid, neither very congenial. After a few days we moved to the Langham Hotel. I had many kind invitations, including one for a seat and lunch to see the Coronation Procession. I went to Elmwood and to Mrs Olding, and Aunt Carrie scolded me well which I deserve for having been so extravagant. Of course some, but not all, of the relations had to have their say; that is a part of one's punishment. While staying at the Langham Hotel we heard the news of Peace, the liftman, a foreigner, told us.

I went to Middlesbrough in Yorkshire to stay with Dr and Mrs Hedley, Isabel's parents, and once more was with a large family and their friends. They lived at Cleveland Lodge, a rambling two storey house in a large garden with fields, on the outskirts of Middlesbrough as it was then. There were six sons and two daughters, and five of the sons and the daughters were there, also Ivor's tutor, Mr Jocelyn, and another Mrs Hedley and her daughter, Maud, from Toronto. They were cousins, and had to be shown the sights, and I was very kindly taken too. We went to Whitby, Guisborough, Durham, Ripon and Fountains Abbey, so I saw a great deal of that lovely North Yorkshire country from which some of our ancestors came. Spinks from Saithes near Whitby, Storms from Robin Hood's Bay (there are still storms there) and Norton's great or great-great grandmother from Ripon. Middlesbrough was then a hideous dirty mushroom city, with slummy streets and huge ironworks, but once outside the country is very beautiful. The Hedleys loved the old places and were very good 'vergers' like Coey at Winchester, so we saw a great deal. We went everywhere by train, and then walked or had cabs. We also went over the family iron works and saw pig iron in the making. I felt unhappy about the apparent poverty; I had been down a poor street and seen dirty little children with only one garment on. I asked Mrs Hedley about it, and she said that every man in that street was earning about £5 or £6 a week. She was a Guardian - in fact, she was quite the queen of Middlesbrough and knew what she was talking about. She was Welsh, and looked like a Welsh woman, dark, with a splendidly shaped round head, always very plainly dressed, the personification of 'no nonsense''' and so clever and kind - a Low Church angel of kindness. She and Norton took to each other at once (that was ten years later) and she told me that I didn't deserve him, which was very true. Dr Hedley came from Northumberland; he was fair, and 'the' doctor for miles around, and would go to his patients in far off dales in the depths of winter, risking his life through the snowdrifts. He was quiet mannered - but I would rather have disobeyed Mrs Hedley than Dr Hedley. They were wonderful people. I was happy with them and loved being with Isabel and having long talks with her. But it soon came to an end, and one morning all the Hedley family saw me off to Leicester.

I got there in the afternoon and was met by my new mistress and her eldest daughter who was grown up. They were very grandly dressed as they had been to a wedding. We drove in a Victoria three miles to the house. This was quite new, had a long drive and beds of new shrubs and roses. It was not a very big house, the usual 'gabled Tudor' kind, and was furnished with new expensive furniture and thick carpets. Half of it was steam heated - the servants' part and schoolroom and back stairs were left cold. The electricity was made in an engine house near the stables, which also were new and good. There were three horses and a coachman, and a head gardener who lived in the lodge, and had other gardeners under him. Everything was so new, and there were no books or papers about. The drawing room was furnished regardless of expense, and had a wonderful painted grand piano, and there was a conservatory leading out of it which the head gardener kept full of lovely things. It was not used except for 'best'. The family sat in what they called 'The 'All', or in a smaller sitting room off it. These rooms were kept very warm so that often you could not see out of the windows for the steam on them. There was a good wide staircase which the children and I were not supposed to use. My bedroom was really an attic but a nice one, and had a thick soft green carpet which my cold toes appreciated. The drawback to this room was that the box-room led out of it - a space in the roof - and also that it faced north so never got any sun. There was a pretty view of mildly undulating country and an old Tower, part of Lady Jane Grey's home so they said. The schoolroom had some well worn furniture in it, and an upright piano and some old lesson books. The first evening I wondered what to wear and put on an evening blouse and black skirt (a fashion that has come back again) thinking that probably governesses did not wear evening dresses. I found my way to the diningroom and saw that Mrs Z and her daughter had not changed. Their fashion was to change for the midday meal, not for the evening. After dinner that first evening I ate with them in 'The 'All' and we conversed. Mr Z asked me 'Ave you associated much with the Royal Family?' Wasn't that funny to ask the new governess? The two girls were all right, rather leggy and thin as they did not get enough exercise out of doors. They were very backward and had never been to school, so I had plenty to do to get them instructed in everything. The younger one was quick, and was really ahead of the fourteen year old girl, who had the nicer character. I was quite fond of them both and tried hard to teach them all I knew and to open their eyes to things. They were always very good and easy to manage, but when we had our first Scripture lesson I got a shock. They seemed to know hardly anything which was puzzling. I asked at last 'What is Easter?'. The elder had no idea. The younger thought for a while 'I know - it is a Bank Holiday'. 'Have you been christened?' 'Yes, one day before we came here Mother told us to put on our hats and took us to church and we were christened'. 'Did the clergyman teach you anything about it?' 'No'. They were a Baptist family, and had changed to the Church of England when they changed to the new house in the country when Mr. Z got so rich. They had never had any Christian Instruction except what they had picked up. Now my own religious belief had gone through a worrying period when I was twenty, I seemed to have so little faith and to feel 'what is the good'. What kept me from falling away was remembering that my relations and my friends believed, so there <u>must</u> be religion, even if it did not seem to reach to me. So I went on going to church and this faithless time did not last long. It has made me understand that young people can have genuine doubts. The Dockyard chapel and chaplain were not helpful, but we had had every chance, so I ought not to have been affected by that. The chaplain had dirty nails, and the chapel was hideous. At Leicester we all went to Matins on Sunday, and once a month 'stayed' for Communion, at least Mrs Z and I did. The children and I walked across the fields to the village church, and the others drove in the carriage. I liked the walk for I did not get out enough. I took the children to a dancing class In Leicester once a week and got to know my way about the town. It was so clean for a manufacturing city, and another thing that struck me was that even the main streets were paved with knobbly cobbles which were uncomfortable to walk on. Hosiery and boot making were, I think, the chief manufactures. One saw poor people pushing old prams laden with white stockings and I was told the seams were sewn in the cottages. In the cottages of our village we could hear the noise of tackety tackety machines, which they said were machines for putting fancy stitching on shoes and boots. Miss Z, the eldest daughter, went to Germany soon after I arrived, and her Mother made a companion of me and wanted me to be with her a great deal when we were not at lessons. She took me to two big balls, at one of which, the 'Tennis Ball' she was the Official hostess. They were held in a fine room with a specially built dancing floor, and had a marvellous band from London. I had lots of partners, for Mrs Z was kind about that, but it was all so different. At one dance the county came, and town and county did not mix. Of course I was Town. County danced the Lancers in the romping 'kitchen' way to which I was accustomed; Town danced them like a dancing class, so County got rather in the way. My partner complained to me of the dreadful way that the County people danced and I had some difficulty in politely agreeing with him! I was also taken to help at a big three day bazaar. It was quite a grand affair, with a Guard's Band playing, and opened each day by an important person. I made friends with two girls at a nearby stall who were helping Lady '…..' Admiral Morant's sister. She asked me to spend a Sunday with her, but Mrs Z. would not let me go. Margaret Spittal was Matron at the Convalescent Home at Loughborough, and she also asked me to go and see her, but Mrs Z would not allow that. Aunt Nora came to Leicester for a few days, and I saw her and prowled with her about some of Leicester's old buildings while the children were at dancing class.

I once had an afternoon and evening to myself and walked back from Leicester after leaving the children somewhere, and was really free for a few hours. That was the only free time I had from the beginning of August until the middle of March when I left the Zs. They had a grown up son who was at home, a weak youth of about eighteen who was a disappointment to them. Mrs Z used to speak as if she hated him; she always nagged and nagged at him if he was in the room. He could not be left alone. He had what she called low friends, which was probably true. I found out that he had a pretty tenor voice and used to encourage him to sing, and learnt all his accompaniments, so many evenings he would stay in instead of wandering about. I never knew half what was wrong and never liked to ask. They packed him off to Canada to get rid of him and he was delighted to go. During the War I noticed his name in a New Zealand casualty list among the killed, and think that it was probably him. The eldest daughter was not her parents' joy either. She was plain, but if she had smiled that would not have mattered. She always seemed so sulky and disgruntled and preferred being in Germany. Lots of relations used to come to the house for occasions. There was a brother-in-law who was a commercial traveller who used to recite - I liked him. It was the low point of view about everything that one had to endure that was disagreeable, finding Mr Z listening outside the maids' bedrooms when I had had my evening bath and wanted to get up to my room; my letters being opened, curiosity about everything, maids being rude to their mistress, oh dear, it was all so common. I had never heard that awful word 'uplift' then, but it was what I honestly tried to do. At Christmas time I determined not to get homesick, and coached the children and some of their cousins for a play which had several songs in It. I made the dresses and did the scenery and was prompter and orchestra and it was fun for us all. On Christmas afternoon I dressed up as Father Xmas, knocked at the front door, and the son and I dragged in a washing basket full of presents for all the family and relations in 'The All'. Mrs Z of course was the giver of the presents and knew the secret. I did meet one interesting person there as well as the commercial traveller uncle, and that was Sir Oliver Lodge, who stayed for a night when he came to give a lecture. He was very benign looking and had an enormously high bald head. When they had all gone to the lecture the housemaid called me to his room and showed me a large night cap in Jaeger flannel! I found that Norton had one of these things to keep his bald head warm on cold nights at sea, and insisted on his giving it away even though Sir Oliver Lodge wore one too! They look like a jelly bag and are hideous. Norton got Nannie King to crochet him a little round cap instead!

I left Leicester in March 1903 and went to Meck. That evening, when they began to ask me questions about my experiences, Dolly stopped them and said that disagreeable things are better blanked out of one's memory and not talked about. She advised me to blank out all that I could. And she was quite right, I can remember the nasty bits if I try to, but from that day to this I have never let myself dwell on it. Uncle Blomfield said that he thought I preferred Meck and the *anciens pauvres* to the *nouveaux riches!*

I learnt two very useful things while I was with the Zs. One is that maids and governesses must have regular times 'off' and holidays. One half day in eight months taught me this very thoroughly! And another is to pay wages and salaries regularly on fixed dates. I could never get my salary without asking for it, which made me horribly uncomfortable. Remember that I had no money since the May before, except for a very kind present from Tem and for a loan of £5 from a society that Dolly knew about and which had to be paid back as soon as possible after one got work. Train fares, washing, stamps, Church collection etc. used up this money during those months while I waited to go to Leicester. The Registry Offices also take a large fee for getting you work. I have purposely not mentioned any names of people or places in Leicester as I don't think it honourable.

The Coronation

I had not seen any of the family for a long time. Kate was a good correspondent and wrote me long letters, especially a splendid one describing the Coronation Procession of King Edward the August before. Father and Marian had seats in the Nave of Westminster Abbey, and Marian and Louie were still luckier for they were among the Peers. At the last moment four seats could not be used, and Naval officers drew lots for them and Harold won! He dashed to town and got Louie. She could wear her wedding dress but had no feathers and all the shops were shut -

however Lyddy Morant came to the rescue with some. We were all so glad that Harold and Louie had that wonderful treat. When I got back to town in March 1903 Father was not at The Warren but had leased a house in North Kensington, Esmé had gone to Spain and Kate and Rose were with him and Marian. They had left Devonport the summer before and had been abroad. They were always moving about. Either that summer or the one before they went to Court and Marian and Kate were presented. Kate was photographed afterwards by Speight for a Court photograph; it is a good likeness. The veil and feathers always make people look different. She wore my old French pendant and also one of my bracelets. The pendant is the one that I have given to Phyllis and which she wore at her wedding.

To the Philipps' family as Governess in Pembrokeshire

Amroth Castle

Once more I had to tackle a registry office for a position for I wanted to remain independent. I was offered one which was too alarming for shy me to tackle. A Mr Calvert, who had married a Greek princess, wanted a governess for his daughter of fifteen, and also she would have to supervise the behaviour and table manners of his little boy of four. During the summer they lived in a palace on the Dardanelles. The journey there by sea would be paid for if you remained for three years. He wrote long instructions about it all, and wanted a photograph of any suggested women. The office sent my photograph, but I said I did not want to go. Suppose I got ill, or hated it, I should be stranded in Turkey. Also the salary, £30 a year, was too low to make one willing to risk going there. Mr Calvert kept the photograph (which made us smile) and wrote asking for me at slightly easier conditions, but I definitely refused and went on looking for a suitable post.

I went to stay at Elmwood and heard from the registry office of a Major and Mrs Ivor Philipps who wanted a governess-companion for their only child. They were living just then at Amroth Castle in Pembrokeshire, and an interview could be made with Mrs Philipps' sister Mrs. Burgess. Aunt Carrie took me to town to meet Mrs Burgess, who was pretty and pleasant and advised me not to go to her niece as she was such a naughty child! However we all liked each other and Mrs Philipps wrote to me to come. Uncle George looked up Major Philipps and Amroth in his reference books, and all was as it should be, so off I went on the long train journey to South Pembrokeshire one lovely day, early in May 1903. Now began one of the happiest times of my life, indeed a 'shower of blessing' was living with Mrs Philipps. She is an angel of kindness and wisdom, so gentle and so witty and it was heaven to be with her after what I had been through.

I arrived at a tiny station, so small that one thought the train was stopping for nothing, and I was admiring a dogcart and two horses out of the train window when the guard came to tell me that I had arrived - and the dogcart was for me. Then came a few miles driving up and down steep hills, which these strong horses took as easily as flat country, in beautiful fresh air, the only houses little white or pink or blue washed ones - a steep hill down to the sea, a little village called Amroth, then a gate where a child was waiting. She climbed up and sat between me and William the groom. She talked hard and stared at me and we drove along the drive which was a long arch of trees which had been blown right across by the sea wind. Amroth Castle had first been built in William Rufus' time, and the front floor and hall and the drawing room and dining room to right and left were very old, but there were big modem windows in the enormously thick Walls. Mrs Philipps was young and gentle and seemed rather shy, just like she always did, and gave me a kind welcome, and Marjorie had a good look at me and showed me my room and the schoolroom. There was nothing 'grand' and no electric light. We had lamps and candles and I felt relaxed and happy. The second morning at lessons Marjorie started the tantrums, and when lessons were over at 12 and I went into the garden, I expected to get the sack, but instead Mrs. Philipps apologized for the naughtiness. I did not know what had upset the child and think she was just trying it on with the new governess. After that I never gave way, and we became great friends. We did everything together, long walks, helping to look after chickens, playing on the sands and hunting for prawns in the rocky pools, and driving about the lanes in the governess cart with Holly the welsh pony, always accompanied by Rags the Welsh terrier. The little church of St Elidyr was at the top of the hill, and the service was in English as that part of South Pembrokeshire was 'colonised' hundreds of years ago (1300 and something?) by Flemings. There is a similar colony at The Mumbles near Swansea, Pembrokeshire - in fact all Wales was ringed with Castles by the Normans to keep 'the wild Welsh' in order. They are still there, not a bit wild, speaking their own language, singing their lovely music, with their own National Anthem. The Flemings are still there too as they did not intermarry. They are a fair people like you see in North Germany, and walk stumpily, and they talk a singsong English like the Welsh do when they speak English, only not quite so much so. Quite close to Amroth everyone spoke Welsh. Marjorie and I used to try and pronounce the Welsh 'll' but I never could do it, and to say Llanelli is quite impossible for me. The onion boys from Brittany, whom we used to see in Devon and Cornwall selling their strings of onions, came here too and could understand Welsh. A custom that interested me was that every cottage doorstep was ornamented with elaborate designs in white wash. After rain the housewives at once painted their doorsteps again with these curls and twists. We did not know why, but surely it is some very ancient custom. Pembrokeshire has anthracite coal, so everyone burnt it, but in the form of culm. This is river mud mixed with coal dust, and moulded into little balls, smaller than a tennis ball. You make a little fire in the grate, and then pile up the balls of culm rather like those old fashioned gas fires. They get very hot and burn for hours, but you must not poke your fire.

One of the greatest joys of Pembrokeshire is the wild flowers; they grow in masses in that warm damp climate. Pink Primroses come from Saundersfoot near Amroth, and the high banks of the narrow lanes are covered with flowers in the spring, sheets of wild violets and primroses - wild 'stinking' orchids and cowslips growing together, wild columbines, how I loved all those flowers. There were always flowers. We found wild snowdrops in January and the garden flowers lasted on until Christmas. Soon after I got there we went with Mrs Philipps to tea at Hean Castle. The groom William had to go somewhere else, and after tea I was to drive Mrs Philipps to a Railway station as she was going away for the night, and then drive Marjorie home. This rigmarole is to explain why I went to tea too! Mr and Mrs Lewis lived at Hean Castle, and when we arrived Marjorie was taken to the nursery and we to the drawing room, which was full or people. One of them, rather a rough looking man with reddish hair, crossed the room to speak to me and asked in a loud voice 'Are you Mrs Philipps' sister?' 'No, I am the governess' I answered. At once he jumped up and left me. Everyone in the room heard this, and everyone hastily began to talk while I felt like a spot of mud. Afterwards we all walked about the garden and two of the other visitors took me with them, one a very lovely tall lady called Mrs Marjoribanks and the other Lord Gort. We soon left to catch the train. Mrs Philipps never alluded to the man's rudeness but told me he was a queer thing, a Mr

Seymour Allen, who collected house-parties of people he met in town, and they all had to have titles. He was also supposed to swarm up a rope instead of going up his stairs! The Philipps and all their relations were so kind and courteous to me, but one can sometimes get a smack in the eye from other people, and it makes one shy. Norton called that kind of behaviour 'showing the hairy hoof'.

The Philipps family

I have not said who the Philipps were. He was a Major in the British Indian Army, very soon promoted to Lieut Colonel; he had the D.S.O., and had been twenty years in India and in the Chitral and Tirah Campaigns; also D.A.A.G. (or some such alphabet) at the Relief of Peking in 1901.(*This memory is somewhat inaccurate. See Wikipedia for full details. Ed.*) He was the second son of the Rev. Canon Sir Erasmus Philipps of Picton, Baronet, of Warminster, and his Mother had been the Hon. ...... Best. He was one of a large family, all very tall. He was the tallest officer in the Army, 6 ft. 5, beautifully built, not the lanky kind, and very handsome with a charming smile. He had a loud voice and was very keen and interested in all he did. The Philipps of Picton are an old Pembrokeshire family and the baronetcy is a James I one, but the ancestors date back to old Norman and Welsh times. Sir Erasmus was not well off, and through a long chain of what I can only call queer doings before the time I was there, the family no longer had possession of Picton Castle near Haverfordwest on Milford Haven. (Picton Castle now belongs once more to the Philipps - one of Marjorie's uncles owns it). His sons were all clever and hardworking; they carried themselves well and some of them have bought land in Pembrokeshire. The eldest son, Member for the district, lived at Lydstep Haven and had two delightful sons who were schoolboys when I was there. Colwyn will be remembered for his poetry and Roland for his work among East End boys. They were both killed in the Great War and their Mother died too. Their father was then Lord St Davids, and he married again and had a daughter and a son. I saw a photograph in an illustrated paper of young Lord St Davids who is very like what Marjorie was as a girl. They are first cousins.

The third brother, Owen, was interested in shipping. He had married a Carmarthenshire heiress, and Amroth Castle belonged to him. He had three daughters, the eldest, Nest, called after an Amroth heroine of 800 years ago. is Lady Coventry whose husband was killed in France? There were two other brothers whom I also met. The youngest was very tall and charming, and was married to a sweet girl, a Miss Speke. He has a title too. Of the sisters I knew Mrs Smallpiece, and stayed with her once at their house on Southampton Water. Her husband was a London doctor, and their child Andrea used to stay with Marjorie and was a delightful thing. Mrs Philipps was the youngest child of another large family. Mr and Mrs Mirrlees of Redleaf, Glasgow, were her parents. She had married very young and gone out to India with her tall young husband. She was not strong, and often had to stay in bed, and used to have bad headaches, but she <u>never</u> talked about it.

After six weeks at Amroth we moved to Cosheston Hall, which they had bought. It is three miles from Pembroke, and the land slopes down through woods to Milford Haven. Marjorie and I drove the fourteen miles to Cosheston in the pony cart in the rain with the baby chicks, all the sticks and crops from the hall, Rags, and the precious baby pheasant, the only survivor of a nest which a mama pheasant had made on a path. We did not know the way but followed the tracks made by the dogcart and carts which had been taking all the luggage and oddments the last day or two. We knew when we had got to Cosheston because the women were standing at their cottage doors curtseying and smiling.

Cosheston Hall

Cosheston Hall had been bought furnished, and the colour schemes were brown and that awful purple red, and nobody would recognize it now. I loved it from the first and wish I could see dear 'Cosh' again. Marjorie and I settled down to lessons and walks, exploring the woods, calling on tenants, making friends at The Vicarage and driving about with Holly. She was given a Sealyham terrier called David and a Persian kitten called Taliesin, and Rags and David only left me when I put them to bed at night. The cat used to come for walks too sometimes. Once a week we drove to Admiralty House in Pembroke Dockyard for dancing classes. At first the Russell's were there but later on came the Dennisons, friends of mine. Their child, Jocelyn, was in one of the dancing classes, a darling amusing child; my Jocelyn is named after her. I used to play the piano for these classes and nobody else would do it. I taught Marjorie piano and singing too, and used to practise both piano and violin. After the dancing lesson kind Mrs Denison would ask me to go upstairs to the drawing room 'and give John his tea' and then Admiral Denison and I would chat until it was time to drive home, while Marjorie played with Jocelyn. The first time we went to the Dockyard the policemen at the gate saluted and passed us in at once, and we wondered if they had been at Davenport Yard gate and knew me. Col. Philipps said they recognised my naval way of driving. It was altogether a peaceful and ideal life for me, living with congenial but reserved people in the country, and I was so happy there. I gave Marjorie all her lessons except Scripture and needlework, which she learnt from her mother. We never spent hours and hours over lessons as even then I thought it was better to work hard and concentrate, and then have lots of time for out of doors. We made friends with the Walkers. Gen. Walker, who commanded the district, had a family of three boys and a girl, and we could go there uninvited; and we knew the villagers and used to pick boxes of wild flowers to send to Aunt Bessy, and drive about all those deep muddy lanes and pull ivy off the trees in the woods, and have all those nice country joys.

Looking back, I can see that the relations must have thought I was rather buried, never having any games or dances nor meeting other young people but, except that I missed Kate, it was a blissful interlude in my life and just what I needed, and living with any Philipps is never dull, they were all so alive and so interested In the world.

Holiday in Switzerland

In the summer of 1904 Father wrote and asked me to join them In Switzerland. I had to reply that I could not afford it, neither the fare nor the hotel bill. I had £50 a year when at Cosheston, and expensive railway fares from Paddington to Pembroke to pay twice a year. I kept strict accounts and never spent more than £25 on clothes. Father wrote again that he meant to pay, so I accepted joyfully. I met Esmé in London, after as usual having a day or two at Meck, and we travelled via Newhaven and Dieppe to Paris. When we reached the Gard du Nord we decided to drive across Paris instead of continuing in the train around Paris. Esmé had been recently in Spain and got her languages all mixed. She talked Spanish to our porter, so I took charge and gave him our hand luggage to take to a *fiacre*. It was quite dusk, lights in the station but not outside, and this may account for me giving him a 20 franc gold piece instead of a franc (then worth 10d). He did not look at his tip but put it straight away in his pocket underneath his blue blouse. Paris still had *fiacres*, like little Victorias, very shabby as a rule, with a bundled up and generally rather bossy driver. We drove to the Gard du Lyon, where I found out my mistake. I always felt that someday I should give a sovereign instead of a shilling tip, and this was at least 16/- only. Father took the mistake philosophically which was noble of him. Esmé and I had dinner at the Gard du Lyon and were amused by some angry English women who knew no French and demanded Milk and Soda from their waiter. He caught the word 'soda' 'Ah oui Mesdames, du visky' and brought them a bottle of whisky. Oh, how cross and indignant they were, the rude creatures. Then someone rushed up to our table 'So you belong to the Polytechnic party?' No, we didn't and we wondered if we looked like that. The Polytechnic used to organize cheap excursions abroad, £7 for seven days to Lucerne and back, and that sort of thing. Esmé had travelled so much, and did not think she needed a conducted tour - although she did mix her languages! We were only four in the second class carriage from Paris to Lausanne, so had quite a good night, awakened at dawn by the train stopping suddenly somewhere in the Jura Mountains. The engine had broken down, very luckily just outside a tunnel. There seem to be hundreds of tunnels in that line through the Juras. We were there some time and it was rather chilly, and some people went for short walks. At last a relief train came and we were packed in and got to Pontarlier, which is the frontier town. Pontarlier was ready for us and there were tables on the platform, and coffee and rolls for us. Esmé and I went for a walk. We did not know if there was anything interesting to see and we found it dull, so went back to the station and after a time our train went on and we got to Lausanne in lovely sunshine. Here we had another railway station meal and then went on in one of those nice clean Swiss trains, so delighted to be back in dear Switzerland, to Sion in the Rhone valley. Oh, the joy of a wash and putting on all clean clothes! I could write reams about Sion. It is a very old town with two steep little hills like sugar loaves in the flat Rhone valley. There is an Archbishop, and in old days it was a very important place. In the little Cathedral there is a <u>very</u> old linen altar cloth, and also a carved and coloured wooden Tree of Jesse which the verger will show you. Next day we started off to Evolène or Evolena if you feel French or Italian. We drove in a little Carriage with two strong horses up and up those zigzags out of the Rhone Valley. It was all bliss to me to see mountains and Alpine flowers again.

Sion in the Rhone Valley

We passed some queer rock formations and the top rocks were more impervious to wind and rain than the rocks underneath, so the top rocks were like umbrellas. I have not explained this well, but believe they can be seen somewhere in the Tyrol too, or in a physical Geography book! We ought to have reached Evolena the night before if we had not been delayed all those hours by the train accident. I telephoned from there to Arolla where Father, Marian, Kate and Rose were waiting for us, to explain what had happened, and the next thing was to find one or two mules to carry our luggage up the steep path to Arolla. We found one, reputed to be a *très mechant mulet* and his old lady owner was dotty, but what did that matter. There was no road to Arolla and I hope it is still roadless, for it is a perfectly lovely place high in the mountains, and cars and tourists would spoil it. There was no village, only two hotels and several cow chalets, a tiny chalet post office where you could buy chocolate, a little R.C. church, and a little English church. It is 6666 feet above sea level, so is snowed in all winter. It is the home of the Arolla pines and of Arolla squirrels which are large black ones. A tearing river rushes from two big glaciers and high mountains tower all around. The Alps are covered with flowers and there are herds of friendly little cows. I say Alps on purpose, because that is what the sloping pastures are called. A rocky path led up to Arolla, which took the newcomer about four hours to walk. The naughty mule took our luggage up quite safely. I was lucky to have strong leather boots given me by Uncle George the winter before. There was an old boot-maker who lived near Elmwood who made wonderfully good boots, and Uncle used to give his friends presents of boots. They were very useful to me in the muddy lanes at Cosh, and when we got to Arolla I had them properly nailed by a guide and always wore them there, and also when we were in Switzerland two years later. I had them for years and years and only gave them away when my climbing days were definitely over. They were not 'blacked' but kept greased with that sticky black grease the guides use.

I have had so many 'showers of blessings' in my life, kindness and goodness all the time, even the Leicester interlude was a blessing although somewhat disguised at the time, but that time at Arolla was a real joy to me. How I loved it all, not the least being with Father and my sisters again after two and a quarter years. We stayed at the Mont Collon hotel, Mont Collon being a great impressive snow mountain towering at the top of enormous glaciers. We had rooms on the fourth floor of the big wooden house, which was very simply furnished with white wood furniture made by carpenters who worked in the open basement; they always seemed to concentrate on commodes or 'night tables' and we wished they would make more chests of drawers! Kate and I shared a room and were very happy doing everything together just as we used to do. On the ground floor there was a big dining room with long tables like a school; a smoking room and drawing room, where a fire was burning when it was chilly, and a glassed in verandah which made a play room in bad weather. There was plenty of good plain food cooked by a Chef in a high cap. He went to bed early and got up at 4 a.m. just when the climbing parties were starting off. There was a sensible arrangement about food for climbers, loaves of bread, raisins, butter, pressed beef and cheese and wrapping paper was left in the dining room overnight. The night porter called you at 2 or 3 or 4 or whenever you wished, you dressed in silence, carried your boots downstairs, had some coffee and a roll and collected your lunch, sat on the floor of the hall and put on your boots - and you were ready. The men carried the food and also bottles of claret. Father always took a flask of whisky 'in case', and once or twice we were glad of it. These early starts were for 'strenuous days' as we called them. On 'loafing days' we started off much later. Sometimes the loaf would turn into a strenuous. We might be picnicking and someone says 'let's go to the upper Arolla Glacier', and all start off for miles. Father liked glaciers best; he always carried an ice axe and loved to cut steps. I liked rock climbing best, and in those days never felt dizzy except when crossing moving water. There were no bridges at Arolla, a log made a bridge over a rushing torrent, and when crossing one I would appreciate someone's hand to keep me steady. Moving water always makes me a bit dizzy, it may be some memory as a baby when living on board the *Implacable*. I never minded heights and precipices, and getting round a difficult corner was a thrill. We walked and scrambled so much that we soon got surefooted; Kate and I would race over the big rock slide at The Pas de Chevres and try to better our time. We never went for the official big climbs as these mean hiring guides and porters which is expensive. Kate and I went up Mont Dolent early one morning, and came down the last slopes on the grassy slide which was dried by the sun. I confess to hating those slippery sides of the small mountain. Slippery grass is treacherous as the grassy slopes so often end in a precipice. There were other young people at Arolla and we used to have tremendous fun. In the evenings Madame would let us take up the carpet in the salon and dance. We were never tired. M and Madame Anzevin managed the hotel and everyone in it, but we were polite to Madame and luckily she liked young English people. They could not bear Germans, and never had them in the hotel if it could be avoided. Some did arrive, the women wearing ghastly 'Nature' (so called) clothes, wool garments from neck to ankle buttoned all the way down, and the mean looking guys, but they had to leave the next day, and another time a party arrived and was sent on in charge of a porter to the nearest hut about 4,500 ft. higher. A porter is a young man who is learning to be a guide. Arolla was a centre for climbing people; they used to come back on Saturdays with their guides and spend Sunday at the hotel, and if the weather were right start off again on Monday. So we were in the midst of climbing talk which entranced me. Our little church was full on Sundays, and while we were there it was consecrated. The Bishop of Northern Europe came for the consecration He was an old man, and it was very difficult for him to get up to Arolla on mule back - and then up a steep path to the church. Esmé and I were in the choir, and also 'did' the flowers while we were there. (The consecration Service was interesting. I was at the consecration of the Roman Catholic Church at Waimate - the services are identical. See Book II) Many of the climbing men were English clergymen having their summer holiday. Father was asked to read the lessons, and when he got to the lectern and saw the congregation he saw rows of round collars! After church he expostulated – 'all you parsons sitting there and expecting me to read the lessons to you!'

I remember how Kate and I were reading Uncle Blomfield's pamphlet about the 'Twenty Two Sayings of Jesus' recently found in Coptic manuscripts, when one of these clergymen came up and asked what we were reading so intently. We showed him the book and he seemed surprised at us. I wish I had a copy of that book now, the only Saying that I can remember is 'Near Me near the Fire'.

Rev. Gurney goes missing

There were all sorts of clergy there of course, a nice Alpine Club one with an Alpine Club son who was in the Army, and a large and noisy Canon Girdlestone who always wore a red tie (Bolshies were not invented then) and another one with thick dark eyebrows, and two quiet thirty-ish daughters. Their name was Gurney. One Saturday evening when we asked Madame Anzevin If we could dance, she refused because Mr Gurney was missing - he had gone out early before his daughters were up and had not returned. All the tired climbers and tired guides spent that night looking for him.

He might have twisted his ankle and been quite close by, hidden by all the tumble of rocks and bushes of roses des alpes. Next morning there was still no news, so Kate and I went to Early Service to pray for him, as we knew girls were no use for this work. When we got home we saw Father just starting off <u>alone</u>, having been sent by Canon Girdlestone to search the crevasses on the Zagazig glacier. We told him to wait for us and rushed to our room and got out of muslin dresses and into skirts and shirts and climbing boots; no time to change out of our thin lisle thread stockings, and as we left we were joined by a young man called Jonas who had arrived the evening before, been out all night, could not bear to stay idle and thought we looked an easy party to be with. Everyone had been questioned as to exactly where they had been the day before, so the search was conducted to certain parts. The daughters thought he might have gone to the Roussettes, a rock mountain, as they had tried to get up it with a guide on the Friday and he had been annoyed not to reach the top. The glacier we were to search was a big one between Mont Collon and Mont Dolent. We methodically went up and down every crevasse, looking for scratches made by boots or stick if he had fallen down one. He had a weak knee, so this could have happened. After hours of this, Father said he was beginning to see a man in a grey suit down each crevasse, so having looked thoroughly we went to the moraine and had lunch, and then put Father on the good path from the Pas de Chevres to Arolla. We young people felt we must go on, so searched the grey shingles slides of Mont Dollent, where we met four young Englishmen doing the same. It was tiring to one's eyes to stare and stare all the time and we were all getting annoyed with people who go mountain climbing by themselves. (We by the way, had seen him for a moment on the Saturday morning as we were having early breakfast before going to the hut above the upper Arolla glacier, 11,000 ft.) Then we said 'let's climb the Roussettes'. It is rather rotten rock and we had a short rope but did not use it. We were surefooted and liked real climbing, and I found a rare flower! We went up and then down one side of the Mountain, and sat down for a rest and to eat the chocolate Father had given us. He always took chocolate with him. We called it 5 franc pieces because each piece was about that size and shape. The sun was getting low and we agreed to chuck it and go home. All the time I remember how Kate was annoyed with Mr Gurney and she was quite right of course. We had some brandy or whisky with us - and Kate said 'I'm sure he is dead and I've brought a large white silk hanky to cover his face'. Kate and Mr Jonas said they didn't know the best way home from where we were, but I knew from the shape of the mountains, and led them straight down, and we got home just before dark. Nothing had been seen of him, and those two poor daughters sat at their bedroom window waiting. The guides went on searching with lanterns, and early next morning a party of men and guides started once more for the Roussettes. They had breakfast where we had rested, and a guide, walking a few yards to one side, found Mr Gurney's body. His knee had twisted and he had fallen from the rocks above.

OBITUARY
The Rev. Dr. H. P. Gurney

A correspondent telegraphs from Arolla under yesterday's date:—'Dr. Gurney, Principal of the Durham College of Science, Newcastle-on-Tyne, in climbing the Gisa, above Arolla, on the 13th, alone, fell from the rocks and was killed instantly. No one knew his plans, so there was little to guide the search parties who went out on Saturday night and Sunday, but his footmarks were observed by a gentleman on Sunday and gave a clue, and early this morning the body was found. There is an English church and churchyard here'. An Exchange Telegraph Company's telegram from Arolla adds that Dr Gurney had been staying there for some time. The body was discovered at the bottom of a gully at the base of the path usually followed for the ascent. Dr Gurney had evidently slipped at the outset of his climb.

We never saw that nice Mr Jonas again, but Kate and I knew how very lucky we were not to have seen that poor body so close to us while we chatted and ate chocolate, and we also agreed together that climbing the Roussettes without a guide had been good but our poor feet were sore after the long day in thin stockings. We always took goggles, scarf, gloves, zinc ointment and a coat with us in our rucksacks, and wore serge or tweed skirts, Viyella blouses and dark bloomers. I once got caught in the rain when wearing a thick cotton blouse and was very sorry for myself. We had gorgeous weather most of the time, but one day woke up to silence, the river had stopped roaring and it was snowing hard. It only lasted two or three days but showed us what a white world Arolla must be most of the year. We went out of course in the snow, and had two picnic lunches in the cold, and tried to melt snow in 'Etnas' to make hot Bovril. Piles of snow make very little water, and then it never seems to boil and everyone gets learned and scientific about barometers and heights. Our time at Arolla was getting to an end, and my holidays were getting over, so back we all walked to Evolène, and next day down to the Rhone Valley, Kate knitting as usual all the time with a ball of wool stuck inside her blouse, and I dashing on ahead, doing a sketch, then dashing on again. I always tried to sketch but could never make a good drawing, although attempting this was great fun. Colour just would not come; I was better at drawing, and yet as you know it is colours that I love. I cannot remember where the family was going to after Arolla. They travelled so much and used to go to Malta for the winter. I stayed a day or two in Lausanne with the Bowrings who lived there then and had been at Arolla. We knew their cousins at Upper Long Ditton who lived close to Mrs Olding. One of the kind people we met at Arolla asked me once 'Why do you enjoy everything so much more than your sisters do?' The reason was that I was having a simply marvellous holiday and they lived most of the time in a holiday. The Bowrings saw me off by the night train from Lausanne to Paris with lots of noise and hurrahs and wavings. I had a carriage to myself and soon went fast asleep and dreamed that I was in an orchard and people were throwing hard green apples at me which hurt. I woke and was still in the railway carriage, covered with bags and suitcases which excited French people were dumping on me. Their train had broken down, so ours was halted and filled up with the passengers. We were packed in and they talked a great deal. A very fat and cross looking woman sat opposite me, so fat that her knees touched mine. I must have slept a bit more, for on waking in the grey dawn in the extremely stuffy carriage (no night air allowed in to hurt French lungs of course) there was the cross woman staring at me, and wearing a silver trinket which Esmé had given me for good luck. My 'nerve' was not equal to hers, so I said nothing. I had a good wash and did my hair and went back to endure the stuffiness. None of the other passengers arranged their toilet at all except a weary looking girl who powdered her very smutty face. We got to Paris and fresh air about 6 or 7 and I drove across to the other station in a *fiacre*. I longed to look at some of my old favourite beauty spots of Paris but was afraid to go alone, so just had breakfast and waited for my train. This time it was full of English people going home after their holiday. One of them asked me if I had heard those noisy people at Lausanne station, and wondered it was allowed etc. etc! Now nobody could stop Bessy Bowring from making a noise if she wanted to, we called her The Duchess because she was so un-duchessey! It was wet and grey when we reached the Channel port so there was the usual quick disappearance of nearly everybody. I had lunch with a climbing Arolla friend - we recognised each other by our rucksacks which we were wearing instead of carrying a bag. It is much easier to have your hands free if you are travelling alone, and also it is rather a protection to look 'sporting' if you are alone on the Continent. I had discovered by now that I was pretty and found it a great nuisance. Being pretty can be a disadvantage if you go about alone. Nobody ever warned me about being followed, and I had some horrid frights which I never dared tell about because I did not understand what it meant, but only felt very frightened and that somehow it must be my fault. I did tell Aunt Bessy years later, and she was so sorry that none of the very kind aunts had thought of warning me. In those days too I was never seasick, not even on a rough Channel crossing, not even fishing right out in the English Channel.

Back at Cosheston Hall

Well, I stayed with Uncle George and Aunt Carrie at Half Moon Street for a day or so and one evening, just as we were dressed for dinner, Marjorie and her father arrived to call, full of apologies at coming at such an hour, but Marjorie was longing to see Jack's Aunt Carrie and Uncle George, just to see if they were real! Aunt Carrie was so amused and liked my bright looking child. I went back to Cosh and once more enjoyed autumn there. October was a perfect month and the trees in the woods sloping to the Haven were gorgeous colours, especially the beeches. We continued our peaceful life, varied with visits to old castles, and when there was a meet nearby Marjorie went to the hunt for a few hours, riding Holly. Sometimes we went to Tenby and occasionally to tea with the Lort Phillips who lived higher up the Haven. They had race horses, including one who had won the Grand National. Mrs Lort Phillips was a Miss Okeover, and I was told had been one of Queen Victoria's maids of honour. The old Queen did not approve of her engagement and threatened to withhold her usual present of a Cashmere shawl and a cheque towards the trousseau, and Miss Okeover curtseyed and said 'I do not need them Ma'am'. It may not be true but it is a nice story.

Miss Maude Okeover was lady in waiting to Queen Victoria from 1884-1887. The shortness of her tenure maybe because she left to get married so there may be some truth in this story.

Characters Maud visited

I confess to being very shy at Lawrenny Castle. They were all very polite but so 'county' and made me shy, and Marjorie knew this. We sometimes went to see the two Misses Mathias, Miss Ada and Miss Rose, who lived at Bangeston near Cosh. They were old maids, known as 'the girls'. We had village friends too. Most of the village men worked in the Dockyard where the minimum wage was 18/- a week. Rents were very cheap, and cottagers could grow their own potatoes and vegetables. The poor wives had to fetch all their water from a spring in the village, and of course the villagers intermarried. I used to call on old Mrs Williams who had a sore leg which she only showed to her friends. I was a friend, but shut my eyes tight when the showing was going on. She had a poor blind son, a man of over forty, who had a fiddle and a harmonium. I tuned his fiddle for him and put on new strings, and he loved to wheeze out hymn tunes on the harmonium while I played his fiddle. He was dying of cancer, but they did not seem to realize it. I did not take Marjorie with me on these visits as the cottage was stuffy and hot; in fact my calls used to come to a sudden end when I felt that one more minute of it and I would be sick. Mrs Williams asked me to go to her funeral 'That will be a real treat for you Miss'. Luckily for Miss, she died during the holidays or else I would have had to go. Poor George Williams died too, and when I met his old father and tried to sympathize, he said that he had done all he could for poor George and bought all the medicines in the advertisements 'George must have drunk over 8 gallons of medicine altogether'. George had a blind cousin, Hester Lloyd, a nice young woman. 'Auntie' had the post office and village store. I never knew her name; she was always called Auntie by the niece who helped her. Poor Auntie found Post Office accounts for stamps a trial, and a worse trial was when the telephone was put in her tiny shop, and she had to manage that complicated engine and telephone on the many wires that were sent to 'The Hall'. Like all the village women Auntie had a long cotton overall, made with a yoke and a waistband, and long sleeves or sleeves to the elbow, of print - it made the women look so tidy.

Colonel Philipps had some tenants whom I used to visit sometimes. There was a genial fat woman who had a weak-minded baby. She would welcome us into the grubby cottage, shoo out the chickens and dust a chair for me. I asked her how many children she had, knowing that there were some grown up ones, and she replied that she was not quite sure if she had buried three or four. Don't blame her, she had a bad husband who got drunk and had hurt the baby. Once when walking by the Haven, we met a gypsy and I walked some way with her. She was about twenty and had a young brother with her, and both were carrying brooms for sale. She was tidy and clean and her hair was braided in neat yellow plaits over her head. I asked her if she did not get tired of never having a home. 'I have got a home, that's our caravan you can see away back there, and we are licensed peddlers from here to Swansea'. I don't think Marjorie enjoyed my visiting, but Tem had brought us up to talk to people and to help them if possible, and Mrs Philipps at that time was not strong enough for these walks.

Carew

One place we went to was a joy, and that was Carew. It is called Care-roo in Pembrokeshire. There is an enormous Norman castle, a great place with four Norman towers, and a Tudor addition which is very tumbledown - smothered in ivy - the enemy of buildings as well as of trees.

Carew Castle

There is also a Celtic cross near the castle – the remains of a moat, and lumpy grass which must cover outbuildings - also a village which had a village baking oven and a large church with a tall tower, a church large enough for a town. And in the church a tomb of a crusader, like the tombs in the Temple church. Only this tomb has a special interest, for the knight's head is too big and is out of proportion and slightly wry-necked. We were sure that this was no sculptor's mistake, but a portrait - if so are all the tombs and brass effigies of the middle-ages portraits? Isn't that interesting?

To Aunt Bessie through the smog of London

I had promised Marjorie to spend Christmas of that year (1904) with her. She was a lonely child and I was very fond of her. A few days before Christmas Dolly wrote asking me to come as she was ill, Aunt Bessy was still very delicate and they needed me to help them and to do their shopping. I left Cosh in lovely weather, flowers still in the garden, and sat with open windows. When the train got to the Thames Valley there was a thick mist, then a thick black fog. The train stopped, crawled on, stopped again, and we were hours late in getting to Paddington. I managed to get a porter and a four wheeler cab, but you cannot imagine what that fog was like. If Mecklenburgh Square had not been on a fairly straight line the cabby could not have taken me. He led his horse, keeping to the curb, and link boys helped us over the crossings and at last we arrived at Meck. I remember that I gave him 10/- which seemed a huge sum to me but I was so grateful to him. I hope he and his horse were able to earn more by Christmas Day, for the fog continued, and all work at the London Docks was held up for a week. And here I must remind you that I am writing all this from memory, I have no books or diaries by me in bed, so it may have been five days for that fog or eight days. It was a horrible fog, which seeps into the house even with every window tightly shut, and makes one feel choky. Aunt Bessy was still up as she never went to bed early, but did not expect me to have been able to leave Paddington station. I did the shopping and housekeeping for them, and then had to go to bed with a chill. The change from Wales to London and from the steam heated train to that cold fog was enough to bring on any chill. Aunt Bessy suffered then from deafness in the middle ear, which made her very dizzy and uncomfortable and Polly was very thin and never very strong; living in London did not suit her.

Christmas in London

We had a happy Christmas with Gertrude and Arthur and Elizabeth, who was six then, and Arthur, and Ida, Susie and Muriel who lived close by. I think it was that Christmas that we had the Chrysanthemum Show. Dolly and I made paper chrysanthemums, arranged them in vases, named them, and put the Christmas presents for each person around their vase. When we all went into the room, everyone had to guess which their particular variety of chrysanthemum was. Tem's was a small yellow one called C. Canariensis (because she liked canaries and kept about twenty of them) and dear Temmy at once got botanical and explained that Canariensis (the climbing plant) had different stamens or something, until we were all laughing so much that she saw the joke. Some rather grubby white ones called 'London Particular' were claimed by Uncle Blomfield, and we all soon found our own flowers. Naming Dolly's and mine had been a bore as we were doing it all, so we called hers the 'Auntie Dahlia' as she was called Auntie Dah by the children, and I was 'The Crimson Rambler'. I forget where I spent the rest of those holidays, but think I was at Elmwood.

Family News

I have given no family news for some time. When peace was declared Helen took Geoffrey to South Africa and lived with Clifford at Standerton in the Transvaal, and her daughter Kathleen was born there. Tom was now I think Naval Attaché at Tokyo. Charlie was always wandering all over the world in different ships; he and May had two lovely curly haired children, Evelyn, Maud and Thomas Sturges, whom May dressed beautifully. She had a little house somewhere north of Finchley. Harold was married, and in the Mediterranean Fleet, and Louie living with Miss Nelson at Putney, where her first child, Betty, was born. Miss Nelson's mother and Sister Annie had both died at the same time, and she was very fond of Louie and the little baby. Esther went on having babies about every eighteen months, I cannot remember if they were still at Penzance or had moved to Alphington near Exeter where they still live. Tem was looking after Grandmother, and of course I always went to see her and Mrs Olding who were both so kind to me.

Last term at Cosheston Hall

I went back to Cosh for my last term there, as Marjorie was to go to a boarding school, St James', Malvern, in May. This school was kept by the Misses Baird, nieces of Admiral Sir John Baird, a great friend of Uncle George's, and it became a famous school. It was started for girls who would otherwise be educated at home with governesses, girls who were used to ladies' maids, and hunting, and so forth. Does this sound snobbish? I don't mean it to be so. Marjorie had always been dressed <u>very</u> plainly and now had to have the St James uniform made for her and it seemed quite grand to us! Navy blue and navy and white chiefly, it must have been one of the first, if not <u>the</u> first, school to have a uniform. It was a very good thing for Marjorie to go away; one could not help treating her as the 'one and only' although I always tried to be more of a companion than a governess.

Off to the Tizards in Bognor

At the beginning of June I went to Bognor to stay with Captain and Mrs Tizard, Devonport friends of ours who had often chaperoned me and were always full of fun. Mrs Tizard was so pretty, she was a niece of the Archbishop of Wales, and her name was Myfanwy, a Welsh name, which her husband shortened to Miff. Captain Tizard was a dear too, and I loved seeing them again. He was then commanding the Sussex Coast Guard station. They showed me the 'sights' of Bognor, which really are impossible to find. It was a small seaside town with a good beach, and the best 'sight' was a crowd of poor London children having a seaside holiday. They took me to Chichester, a lovely old town, where we saw the alms houses in a very old hall like a great barn. Part of the Cathedral was being repaired and visitors not allowed, but naughty Capt. Tizard said I came from New York so we were shown everything. I did not dare speak for fear the verger should not think my accent correct! One day Capt. Tizard hired a car and we drove to Selsea Bill and saw those miles of shingle called Chesil Beach. On the way back the car broke down, back axle broken, so nothing could be done. The chauffeur walked back to Selsea to get us a carriage, and we were asked into a nearby cottage by some very kind and extremely untidy people. Really kind, and they gave us lunch at 3 p.m., and really untidy, the house in a mess, the woman's old cotton dress fastened with safety pins in front, and the man, who spoke like an educated man, had hardly a button on his coat. It was awfully good of them to take in the strangers who had broken down at their gate, but imagine how we felt when we found out that the man was the brother of a retired Commander at Devonport, whose wife and two daughters and he too, could barely know anyone who was not 'county'. We asked the daughters to one of our dances once, out of kindness really, because they were very plain and so haughty and we had difficulty in filling their programmes. Before they accepted the invitation their Mother wrote to ask what other people would be at our dance for she could only allow her daughters to dance with the upper classes. How annoyed Marian was. The Tizards had had a few snubs too. But the poor relations were really kind, although we laughed and laughed all the way back to Bognor when a carriage and pair at last came for us.

Uncle Blomfield dies

Rev Blomfield Jackson prebendary St Pauls 1839-1905

Father: Rev Thomas Jackson MA b: 12 SEP 1812 in Preston
Mother: Elizabeth Prudence FISKE b: 29 MAR 1814 in Berkshire

Marriage 1 Elizabeth Ann 'Bessie' BECK b: 1840 in Stamford Hill, Middx

- *Married:* 1867 in Hackney

Children

1. ♟ Arthur Blomfield JACKSON b: 26 MAR 1868 in Stoke Newington

2. Gertrude Prudence Hamilton Blomfield JACKSON MA b: 13 SEP 1870 in Stoke Newington

3. Theodora Blomfield JACKSON MA b: 10 JAN 1873 in Stoke Newington

4. Sir Gilbert Hollingshead Blomfield JACKSON b: 26 JAN 1875 in Stoke Newington

---

Next morning I had a wire to say that Uncle Blomfield had died suddenly, so had to go at once to Tem and Grandmother. Tem adored Uncle Blomfield. The family said she cried her eyes out when he married and she could no longer do things for him, and we feared that the shock would be dreadful for Grandmother. Uncle Blomfield had had a very short illness. He died of septic pneumonia and was delirious and it was hopeless from the first. He was sixty five, and had always been so strong and well and active, out in all weathers going all over London to preach. He was a Prebendary of St Paul's Cathedral, and as president or chairman of the London Diocesan Reading Union 'belonged' to many things. He was a real scholar but no recluse. He liked to have everything correct in his house, dinner properly served, his glass of sherry, and French beans were always served as a separate course. Many people were afraid of him, no, perhaps that is wrong, they were nervous of him, as his manners were so courteous and his language very highbrow. I loved him and he was so good to me. He took me once to the Chamber of Horrors at

Madame Tussaud's and told me all about every murder! The relations would not believe me, but I knew how murder cases interested him, and how he would buy every edition of the evening papers if there was a female murder trial in England or France. He wanted to know <u>why</u> the murderer had done it; it was not a love of crime. Uncle Blomfield himself was so gentle, but he met thousands of people and wondered <u>why</u> some of them should be so evil.

His house was full of old leather bound books for he could not resist buying them off the second-hand bookstalls in the streets. I used to bring his newspaper cutting books up to date when I stayed at Meck, and also clean the old brass chandelier in the dining room, and help Dolly and Aunt Bessy give the old charwomen who lived in his City parish a treat. He was Vicar of St Bartholomew the Less, Moorfields, until It was pulled down when the tower got unsafe. There were Grinling Gibbon's carvings in that church. He was <u>always</u> the London clergyman, fairly tall 5 ft. 11 in. in a silk top hat, a long beard and a hooked 'Roman' nose. It was all over now, and he had gone after a short but distressing illness. I found Grandmother wonderfully serene, and learnt then that when people get very old sorrows are not so acute. It seemed worse for poor Tem but she was very brave too; it had been such a shock for her. Grandmother was interested in our mourning, and we had to get into the deepest black. I got a dress in Kingston made of black voile with lots of ruchings of the voile, and Grandmother felt it all over and approved of it. The funeral service was at St Pancras Church - that church that has a Greek Portico and pillars.

We left Grandmother in the sensible cook's care, no visitors, and extra treats for her lunch, and Tem and I went by train to Waterloo. I insisted on third class and a crowded carriage, much better for Tem, for I did want to get her through that day without a breakdown. It was a simply glorious June morning. We had plenty of time, so stern niece said we would walk all the way to St Pancras Church. The church was full and I think four Bishops took part. One Bishop preached. It was my first funeral and I felt quite sick, but the job was to keep Tem on her feet. There were some Quakers in the church in Quaker dress, relations of Aunt Bessy. Arthur managed everything and it was all very quiet and no muddles. There were closed carriages and pairs of horses to take relations to Highgate cemetery, and kind Arthur had one carriage for the old granny charwoman from St Bartholomew's parish that used to be. Only one granny had been able to go to the church and she drove in state in a carriage and pair to Highgate - and back to her City slum. I went with Clifford Coffin, my brother-in-law, and Hannah Beck, a niece of Aunt Bessy. We were a queer mixture, and that made it easier for me to bear that drive. I collected Tem again at the cemetery, and afterwards she and Aunt Carrie and Aunt Nora and Father and I all drove back to Half Moon Street to have lunch with Aunt Carrie. Aunt Bessy, whose Quaker calm had fortified her, had had her carriage opened, so we had ours open too which was better for us. Tem was a stalwart that day and through the time that followed. Grandmother wanted to be told all about everything, and the only time

I found her really upset was when an old clergyman came to see her. I was only a squirt of a granddaughter so couldn't prevent him going to her room - after some time he came down and said he thought he had comforted her and had repeated her favourite hymns to her. We rushed upstairs with a glass of port for poor Grandmother. She was then ninety-one. Aunt Bessy and Dolly had a great deal to do, so for a few days I went to Meck and helped them. Gilbert was in India and Aunt Bessy asked me to copy some of the condolence letters into an exercise book. Marjorie copied our letters when Norton died, so I know what the strain was. At first you feel you cannot bear it - and after a few days you find yourself almost criticizing the grammar. I said almost. One telegram came from 'Charles' and Aunt Bessy and I did not know that Charlie was in England but thought how nice of him to wire. But why sign himself Charles? and Aunt Bessy, looking again, saw the postmark was Windsor Castle and 'Charles' was Prince Charles of Denmark now the King Haakon of Norway who had married Princess Maud of Wales. The Princess Louise had written and sent a wreath, asking for it to be put on the coffin, and I think Princess Victoria wrote and sent flowers. There were columns about Uncle Blomfield in all the London papers. One morning we were working in the little room near the front door when someone came to see Aunt Bessy. They went upstairs to the drawing room and were there a long time. At last Aunt Bessy came back and we asked who it was. 'I don't know' she said, but she cried and was so much upset about Blomfield, so I gave her some sherry and tried to comfort her. It was funny, but oh how I admired Aunt Bessy's unselfishness. There was a Buckingham Palace garden party that week to which Father and Marian had been invited, and Marian had a new pink dress and hat for it. She was told that she simply could not go to the party, suppose Father was seen by one of the royalties, how horrified they would be. Father and Aunt Bessy were great friends and he often looked in at Meck during that first sad day and told Aunt Bessy of Marian's disappointment. 'Nobody would have sympathized with her more than Blomfield, who so loved the royalties' she said.

I stayed with Mrs Olding, so still saw Tem and Grandmother as Fresno was only three miles away. I remember lunching with the Hedleys one day and going with Isobel and Walter in a hansom to Ranelagh where there was some big day. It was crowded with smart men and ladies in long trailing dresses, and how pretty Ranelagh looked! We joined another party there, and I met a man who completely silenced me for conversation although after all these years of meeting strangers I thought I could prattle to anyone. This was not shyness, just being taken absolutely aback, for he said 'I live all the year for Henley Sunday in the Park, just to see the lovely dresses'. Now what can you say to that, or at least what could one in those days say to a complete stranger? Isabel must have seen my face, and came and rescued me from the dress lover.

Holiday in Anglesea with the family

All this time I had not joined the family and it was arranged that we should all meet at a London station and go to Anglesea for some weeks, where Marian had taken a seaside cottage she had seen advertised. The party consisted of Father and a tin dispatch box that he seemed to treasure, Marian and a great deal of hand luggage, Kate, Rose, now a pretty thin child of nearly eleven, too nervous and always in a panic that Father would be left behind if he got out at a station; Nelly Evans, the eldest niece who was 6½, three bicycles and me. We got as far as Chester the first day and Father and Kate and I did some sightseeing. I can't describe Chester, it is unique, and is all a dull pink sandstone. The Cathedral is quite pink. When we were shown the Cathedral by the Verger, there must have been a Protestant in the little party of sightseers, for when we were shown what would have been the chantry over the tomb which had been smashed by Cromwell's men, I said to Father 'Oh, wasn't that wicked' which called down a storm of abuse from the Protestant. I kept very quiet after that. It is a strange mind that thinks it a virtue to destroy churches or beautiful things in churches. Chester is full of history and you think of Saxons and King Charles I and all your English History. Next day we went on to Anglesea, looking forward to bathing and paddling. We went over the Menai Bridge and then on to flatter country, and got out at a little station which was a short walk from our cottage. Not a sign of the sea! We asked where it was - three miles away! We had been completely duped, but still, there we were.

It was a modern two storey little house on the dusty road, with no garden and no shade, the most unattractive and dreadful little place. Still there we were, so we unpacked and had some sort of a tea meal provided by the rough young woman who was to 'do' for us. I could not sleep for the fleas, and next morning was bitten all over. We had all been bitten but I was the show piece; Kate caught 40 fleas in my bed - and fleas jumped about the tablecloth at meals - we killed lots, and put Keatings everywhere, but fleas still feasted on me and I felt wretched. We bicycled to Holyhead, and also to the nearest beach, a really lovely bit of coast, very rocky with a sandy beach and a good hotel which was full so we could not move there. Anglesea is windswept like parts of Cornwall, and there seemed to be very few trees in the north or west of it. The fleas were impossible and so was the landlord when protests were made. Father went to Bangor to find a solicitor to ask his advice, as the cottage had been taken for a month, and he took me with Kate as a 'show piece' for I looked horrible, bitten all over. The solicitor was kind and said they wanted to let their house for two or three weeks and we could go there - which we gladly did the next day. We went for long walks and bicycle rides and had lovely bathing in that perfectly lovely part of Wales. We went to Beaumaris one day and saw a comical epitaph in the churchyard beginning 'Pray stop your fool'; the stonemason evidently only spoke Welsh and had been given some English to carve and did not bother about it. One sunny afternoon Kate and I went to Llanfair...P...G. The place with the longest name in the world is shortened to this on the signposts and in speaking of it.

It has ever so many syllables and ends with 'gogogoch'. There was a little island, the quietest little green island with a few beautiful trees, where both Kate and I thought we should like to be buried. We saw it in the setting sun and we never forgot its peace. Kate is buried at Cairo and I suppose I shall be buried in Norton's grave, and of course it does not matter really where your body rests, but that little island was our choice. And I think it was at Beaumaris that we saw a large statue of the Marquis of Anglesea (below) who lost a leg at the Battle of Waterloo, and had his leg carefully buried there.

We found its tomb in 1927, but I hope to write about that later. Father was so amused with this extraordinary fact that it impressed me too, and made me search for it when we went to Waterloo in Belgium, I say 'in Belgium' because Waterloo always means the station to me! Then we went to wonderful Carnarvon Castle, and beautiful Conway Castle, and inland among the mountains. Kate and I would go for miles and miles and loved being in hill country again. One day we all went off to see a waterfall called Aber. We expected a nice little splashy trickle, all of us having seen great waterfalls in Switzerland. Aber was a surprise' It really is a fine fall and we all got very enthusiastic about it and went again to see it. There is a lonely lake called Llyn (lake) Ogwen, dark and gloomy, and beautiful little lakes, and slate mines near Bethesda. We did not know why such a name! We sat on the hillside opposite the slate mine watching the work for a long time. Bethesda is interesting too. It has a University, and a small Cathedral to which we went; the service was a mixture of Welsh and English and the singing good. There was a pleasant maid left in the house that tried to teach us to say Eisteddfod with no success, and told us about it, and about how hard everyone practises their part singing. Welsh songs are lovely and yet how seldom one hears them. Marjorie and I had a book of Welsh songs and learnt several of them. Neither of us could sing but that did not matter much. We learnt the National Anthem 'Land of Our Fathers' in Welsh, a glorious tune. Marian used to call it 'My Hen That Would Fly' because in Welsh the first words are 'Mae haen gwlad fwn laddau' - oh dear, I cannot remember how to spell it now.

To go back to Bangor, we enjoyed the bathing there in an open air swimming pool of sea water which was submerged at high tide. Rose was a dear little person, but Nelly was so naughty, at least she was naughty when with Kate and me. Marian had almost adopted her and was so kind and patient with the child. Nelly was always on the defensive and making the worst of herself, but Marian understood her and she practically got what I call softer. Marian sent her to school later on and afterwards to the Royal Naval School for Officers' daughters near Richmond, and Nelly as a schoolgirl, when I saw her there, was a very nice friendly and prettily mannered girl.

From Bangor we went to stay at Colwyn Bay, which is east of Bangor and is a regular seaside place. We could see Llandudno in the distance but never went there as we were told it was a sort of Blackpool. Colwyn Bay was supposed to be grander. There were very good sands where Father, Kate and I worked hard at building fortifications for the so-called amusement of the little ones! By the way have I mentioned the toy railway that Father gave to Rose? We used to put it out in a big room; I can remember it all over the hall and passages at Devonport. I was Traffic Manager and it took two hours to fit all the rails and points together. There were three steam engines. Father and Tom were General Managers of the Railway Company, and sometimes we would have an accident on purpose, for them to study the results. Rose was not allowed to touch it as she might have burnt her little fingers - she was allowed to look on! The engines were filled with methylated spirits and had real steam whistles. Here I am wandering again, but that railway of Rose's always amused me, and the Colwyn Bay forts were like it. There are beautiful places inland from Colwyn Bay, each like an artist's dream. Everyone has heard of Betws-y-Coed, which is lovelier than anyone could describe, although every tourist in North Wales goes there. We had it to ourselves the day we were there. A strange thing happened to me there. I was going down some rocky steps quickly, ahead of Kate. and trod on a snake that must have been sunning itself on the rocks. I hurt it with my heel, but it escaped down the steps. It was a nasty experience. Father wanted to know which was the more surprised, the snake or Seagull! (He always used our nicknames). One day we went to a wonderful old house, I think the name is Llanrust - in the same kind of lovely wooded hilly country. There was a high wall along the lane, with a door in it. Father rang the bell, and handed in his card and asked if we might see the house. The housekeeper came, and showed us all over an ancient house like a story book. The garden had rows of yews which she said were 700 years old. The rooms of the house were panelled, the ceilings wooden too, and all almost black with age. One bedroom had an old dark four-poster bed in it, and dark carved chests, and this she said was the haunted room. Hundreds of years ago two brothers (or perhaps it was two friends) had fought a duel in this room for a lady. The incident had not been witnessed. One man was killed and the other hid his body behind the wooden panelling - and here the housekeeper showed us the spot. It was a mystery as to what had become of the murdered man. But people who slept in that room heard the sounds of swords as if there was a duel in the room. Here Father, the ever practical, said 'Of course nobody in those days had a sense of smell'. We were all sure that apart from duels and hidden bodies we should not like to sleep in that gloomy room. We were shown the saloon, which was chock full of furniture, much of it with a history, including some of Mary Queen of Scots' fine embroidery, and Coronation chairs. And then we were taken to two cheerful modernized bedrooms, with rosy wall papers and plenty of light, and these rooms the housekeeper said were used by the Duke and Duchess of York during their honeymoon (King George V and Queen Mary). I think she said they were there for two days.

We made an expedition to St Asaph, which is in the flatter country bordering Cheshire; it is only a village but as it has a tiny Cathedral is called the City of St Asaph. Marian wanted us to see it as her sister Mrs Sisson lived near there during her married life. We left Wales soon afterwards and I do not remember where I went first. Esmé must have been training as a nurse then, she was not with us in Wales and must have been at Queen Charlotte's Hospital. It was very hard work there, and she used to look very thin, but pretty. The nurses' hours were very long. We went to see her in the Hospital, and met her patients and saw some darling babies. Slum babies can be just as sweet as rich ones, and some of them just as comical. Esmè liked the work, although none of the nurses can have liked going out by themselves to cases in the poor homes - that must generally be very difficult, but Esmé had lots of grit and stuck it out. Helen and Clifford and their two children were living at Ealing as Clifford had an appointment at the War Office for some years. Helen was expecting again, and used to stay indoors all the time. She looked tired but did not seem to be ill and <u>we</u> thought she ought to get fresh air, but did not say so, as Helen hardly mentioned the new baby to me.

Once more I stayed with Tem and Grandmother, and Tem was able to have a holiday. It was a cold autumn and winter seemed to come very early. One morning In October there was 15 degrees of frost, and everything in the garden was blackened and dead. I always hated cold and winter and dark days and in the Thames Valley there are also fogs which choke one. Fresno was quite close to the Thames in a quiet road with big trees overhanging it, and used to feel very damp. My allowance from Father was £25 a year, the same as Kate and Esmé had, and this had to pay for all clothes, pocket money and train fares. You will perhaps like to know how I dressed. I had had two coats and skirts made by a good little tailor in Tenby and this autumn went to a tailor called Dale, north of Regent's Park, and ordered a thick black coat and skirt, the coat three quarter length. His usual price was two pounds two shillings, but for a special coat and skirt like this one of good material and a black velvet collar, he charged three pounds and three shillings. He had a huge number of customers and one only had one fitting. I had a large brown rainproof coat which had some wool in it, which was warm enough for Pembrokeshire. I made my own shirt blouses, and could re-trim a hat. Only once did I succeed in trimming a hat for myself which was becoming, and yet I could make hats for other people. I made toques for Tem and Mrs Olding quite successfully, beginning with the wire frame. There was a fashion for paper hats, and these I could make too out of rolls of crinkled paper. You cut the roll into narrow strips, plaited them like a straw plait, and then made up the hat. I always liked sewing but was stupid at dressmaking and afraid of wasting the material. One could buy black woollen stockings for two shillings and sixpence, and in summer we wore lisle thread openwork ones which were also cheap. Shoes were a difficulty. You could get a pair of black glacé house shoes with lowish heels and black ribbon bows for seven shillings and sixpence, and I used to try and make a pair last a year. We wore nainsook chemises and drawers and nightgowns. I bought three nainsook nighties at a 'White sale' for one pound, which I thought a bargain and they wore very well. I had a hot water bottle, because soon after I arrived at the place near Leicester a parcel arrived with a big tin hot water bottle, one ought to say can rather, sent by our second housemaid at Devonport hoping that Miss Maud would not be cold as she knew how she feels the cold. That was yet another of my showers of blessings - and wasn't it kind of Stephens? I always tried to be very neat. Of course there was no money for evening dresses, but I had two old ones from 1901 and the pink evening coat that Tom and Harold gave me one Christmas about 1900, which was the height of fashion. I had had no winter coat. Corsets were a very small expense as I was thin and only needed a belt thing with suspenders which cost about three shillings and sixpence. We used to watch the advertisements and try to buy what we needed at sale time.

And now I am going back to Fresno and that chilly early winter. It was not very lively there; even Tem used to get awfully bored and longed to get away for holidays. When one of the relations came it was nice; especially Aunt Carrie who was Grandmother's favourite visitor too. Nobody in the district ever came near us. I used to think it very queer of the Rector of the Parish (Teddington) that he never came to see Grandmother, a widow of a clergyman and one of the oldest parishioners. Uncle Blomfield gave her Holy Communion and after his death, one of the curates came. I liked going to Teddington Church which was gay and bright and well warmed. It was high which is what I like, and the singing of the Gregorian chants was beautiful. The church was not finished then, only half of the nave had been built, so there was an extraordinary custom there at sermon time of everyone who sat further east than the pulpit getting up and turning his chair round to face the pulpit. A dreadful noise before and after the sermon was the result. Another noise in that church was rather funny, and that was the silk rustlings of the entire well-to-do suburbanite women as they walked up the church. Dresses were lined with silk and they also wore the most elaborate and rustling taffeta petticoats too to church - so the effect was much more than a froufrou. That church was a real centre of the parish, and I liked the way that the youths of the parish were put into red cassocks and given something to do in the church, as altar servers, or carrying banners - for there were lots of poor people in Teddington as well. For early service we used to go to a tiny plain church close to Fresno, called by Kate 'Tem's Tin Tabernacle' where a curate celebrated. My great joy at Fresno was being only 3 miles from Mrs Olding, and about 1½ miles from Hampton Court which I know in all weathers and at all times of the year. It was a pretty walk across Bushey Park to Hampton Court, or one could walk to the end of Kingston Bridge and go by tram. Electric trams were everywhere then and motor cars quite common. Grandmother told me that people complained to her that motors were noisy and made a dust and were dangerous and spoilt the look of the country. 'Exactly what people said about trains when we first had them' said Grandmother! We had many talks together, and she liked to be read to, which was hard on the reader as you had to read Sir Walter Scott into her right ear. Poor dear, she sat there alone in her blindness. 'Tell me something' - and my mind would go blank. Sometimes I bought a paper called M.A.P. (Mainly about People) which consisted of quantities of short paragraphs about wellknown people; this was kept on my lap and came in very useful to amuse Grandmother. While Tem was away I slept in a little room next to Grandmother, who prided herself that she never called me. But I would hear bumps and rush in to her without bothering to put on a dressing gown, and find her fumbling for her water or something. She was always so glad to have you there 'but I didn't call you did I?' The nights must have been long for her. She was not a good gentle old lady but we really were friends. She had such strong likes and dislikes and used to say what she thought.

After Tem came back I went to stay with Mrs Olding and told her that I did not feel very well and had some sort of rash on my chest. She took me to her doctor who said it was a form of nettle-rash, and put me on a diet of bread, butter, cheese, milk and potatoes. The rash went but I still did not feel very fit; however I stuck to the diet. Once when out at lunch the only thing I got was one boiled potato! Mrs Olding being Devonshire thought that good nourishing food would be better for me, but we felt the doctor must know best. Next I went to Elmwood where such a diet was not tolerated. Elmwood was always so warm, fires in the bedrooms, even a fire in the hall, so the whole house felt cosy although there was no central heating. One day we went to Guildford with Uncle George's sisters Ellen and Edith Beck, and drove in an open carriage to see King John's Lodge at Shere which had been inherited by the Fraser-Mackenzie's of Bunchrew, Inverness, great friends of Uncle George's and Aunt Carrie's. In fact, they were Uncle and Aunt to them, and we girls used to think Mr Bob Fraser-Mackenzie rather an elderly cousin. Phyllis met them when she first went to Tulloch, and was told that they had known her since before her birth. They have both died recently, such dear people. This old house we went to see was supposed to have been a hunting lodge of King John, and it was haunted. During the Great Plague a man went there from London with his daughter. She died there of the plague, and as everyone had left him, he had to bury her himself and had to drag her body down the winding stairs. The 'haunt' is that people hear a heavy weight being dragged down the stairs. It was a grey December day, and a very cold drive back to Guildford. Kate had knitted me a grey woollen hug-me-tight which I wore under my black coat and skirt, but it did not keep the wind out.

Soon after this I went back to The Warren, where we were all to spend Christmas. It was years since I had been there and I felt a stranger, but it was lovely to have a family Christmas again after four years. I was keeping my promise to Mrs Philipps, but always preferred a settled life. However, I knew now that I could earn my living even though Dolly considered it wrong to earn money if anyone else could support you, or you had a private income.

Then came New Year's Day of 1906 and I feel it ought to be written in large red letters, for this was the year that Norton and I met and were married.

END OF PART ONE